Endorsements

"It's a real gift to the church when a seasoned theologian, with insights gained from years of personal experience and biblical study, handles a tough topic like suffering. Here you will find the wisdom of biblical perspective combined with the eternal hope of the gospel leading you to greater rest in your Savior, even in times of trouble. I am thankful for the new edition of this book."

—Dr. Paul David Tripp
President, Paul Tripp Ministries
Philadelphia

"As an oncologist, I have the privilege of caring for people as they 'walk through the valley of the shadow of death.' In such times, people of faith find themselves faced with the most troubling questions of human existence, namely those raised by suffering and death. In *Surprised by Suffering*, R. C. Sproul concisely and sensitively affirms what I believe to be the three critical truths we need to grasp in order to persevere through suffering and death. First, the inevitable and vocational nature of death/suffering; second, God's sovereign redemptive purposes in suffering; and finally, the certainty of eternal life in perfect fellowship with Him and our fellow believers. I was delighted to learn of this book's republication, and my reading of the manuscript reaffirmed why we do not grieve as those who have no hope."

—Dr. James W. Lynch Jr.
Professor of medicine
Division of Hematology/Oncology
University of Florida College of Medicine, Gainesville, Fla.

"In *Surprised by Suffering*, John Calvin meets Florence Nightingale. This is a rare work, a melding of the theologian and the pastor—a book that looks straightforwardly at suffering and teaches, explains, confronts, and comforts. Buy a dozen, as you will be giving this one away to someone who is hurting in the world around you."

—Rev. John P. Sartelle Sr.
Senior minister
Christ Presbyterian Church, Oakland, Tenn.

SURPRISED
BY SUFFERING

SURPRISED
BY SUFFERING:
THE ROLE OF PAIN AND
DEATH IN THE
CHRISTIAN LIFE

R. C. SPROUL

IR *Reformation Trust*   A DIVISION OF LIGONIER MINISTRIES, ORLANDO, FL

Surprised by Suffering: The Role of Pain and Death in the Christian Life
© 2010 by R.C. Sproul

Previously published as *Surprised by Suffering* (1988) by Tyndale House Publishers.

Published by Reformation Trust Publishing
a division of Ligonier Ministries
421 Ligonier Court, Sanford, FL 32771
Ligonier.org   ReformationTrust.com

Printed in Crawfordsville, Indiana
LSC Communications
0000320
First edition, sixth printing

ISBN 978-1-56769-184-9 (Hardcover)
ISBN 978-1-56769-218-1 (ePub)
ISBN 978-1-56769-967-8 (Kindle)

Cover design: Gearbox Studios
Interior design and typeset: Katherine Lloyd, The DESK

All Scripture quotations are taken from the New King James Version®. Copyright © 1982 by Thomas Nelson. Used by permission. All rights reserved.

Library of Congress Cataloging-in-Publication Data

Sproul, R. C. (Robert Charles), 1939-2017
  Surprised by suffering : the role of pain and death in the Christian life / R.C. Sproul.
    p. cm.
  Originally published: Carol Stream, Ill. : Tyndale House Publishers, c1988.
  Includes bibliographical references and index.
  ISBN 978-1-56769-184-9 (alk. paper)
  1. Suffering--Religious aspects--Christianity. 2. Death--Religious aspects--Christianity. 3. Future life--Christianity. I. Title.
  BT732.7.S687 2009
  236'.1--dc22
                          2009025818

For Alissa Erin Dick,
stillborn infant,
until we meet in heaven

CONTENTS

PREFACE

Those of us who live in Western nations are blessed to a degree previous generations would never have believed possible. For the most part, we enjoy good health, comfortable lifestyles, and security. We do not face imminent threats each day to our existence or even our sense of well-being.

These blessings, however, tend to lull us into a false sense of invulnerability. When we are spared from difficulties over time, we begin to expect that we will always escape hard things. Therefore, if suffering in any of its various forms—disease, injury, grief, loss, persecution, failure—comes upon us, it tends to catch us by surprise. Thus the title of this book.

My purpose in writing this book is that you would *not* be surprised when suffering comes into your life. I want you to see that suffering is not at all uncommon, but also that it is not random—it is sent by our heavenly Father, who is both sovereign and loving, for our ultimate good. Indeed, I want you to understand that suffering is a vocation, a calling from God.

This book was first published in 1988. This new edition features a new chapter on God's sovereignty in relation to suffering (Chap. 4), as well as new Scripture and subject indexes.

It is my prayer that God will use *Surprised by Suffering* to prepare you for whatever valley the Good Shepherd may call you to tread, knowing that He Himself will go with you.

—*R. C. Sproul*
Lake Mary, Florida
June 2009

PART ONE

Unto Death

CHAPTER ONE

SUFFERING, PERPLEXITY, AND DESPAIR

C hristians are those who have faith in Christ. We all aspire to possess a faith that is strong and enduring. The reality, however, is that faith is not a constant thing. Our faith wavers between moments of supreme exultation and trying times that push us to the rim of despair. Doubt flashes danger lights at us and threatens our peace. Rare is the saint who has a tranquil spirit in all seasons.

Suffering is one of the most significant challenges to any believer's faith. When pain, grief, persecution, or other forms of suffering strike, we find ourselves caught off guard, confused, and full of questions. Suffering can strain faith to the limits.

Paul wrote poignantly about his own struggles in times of distress: "We are hard pressed on every side, yet not crushed; we are perplexed, but not in despair; persecuted, but not forsaken; struck down, but not destroyed—always carrying about in the body the dying of the Lord Jesus, that the life of Jesus also may be manifested in our body" (2 Cor. 4:8–10).

The apostle said he was "hard pressed on every side, yet not crushed." He made no attempt to mask his pain in a fraudulent piety. The Christian is not a Stoic. Neither does he flee into a fantasy world that denies the reality of suffering. Paul freely admitted the pressure he experienced.

We all know what it means to be hard pressed. We use the word *pressure* to describe tense moments in our lives. Troubles in our jobs, troubles in our marriages, and troubles in our relationships can mount up and attack our spirits. If we add the tragic death of a loved one or the difficulty of a prolonged illness to these daily pressures, we feel the pain of being hard pressed all the more.

To be hard pressed is to feel as if we are used automobiles that have been consigned to the junk heap and put in a metal compactor. To be hard pressed is to feel a massive weight that threatens to crush us.

When we experience severe heartbreak, we may be inclined to say, "I'm crushed." But this is hyperbole. We may feel crushed; we may even come close to being crushed. But the bold declaration of the apostle is that we are *not* crushed.

We speak of "the straw that breaks the camel's back." I once heard this expression used while attending a Weight Watchers gathering. At the initial meeting for orientation, everyone was given several items, including a food guide, a daily chart for recording what we consumed, an exercise booklet, and a drinking straw. As we neared the end of the meeting and the instructions for the program were completed, the instructor asked, "What made you decide to join Weight Watchers?" Several members of the group volunteered answers. Each person had a different reason: some had seen themselves in recent photographs and couldn't stand the sight; some had had to purchase clothes one size larger; and some had been told by their doctors to lose weight. After this discussion, the instructor held up a drinking straw. "This is your last straw," she said. "This straw represents the reason you decided to join the program. Take it home and put it in a prominent position. Tape it to the refrigerator. When you falter in your desire to lose weight, look at it. Let it serve to remind you of why you are here."

I doubt a camel's back has ever been broken by a drinking straw. The metaphor had its origin in the Middle East, where camels are still used as beasts of burden. The camel is expected to carry straw that is harvested. There is a limit to how much straw a camel can carry. Every camel's back has a breaking point. The difference between a tolerable burden and one that crushes may be a single piece of straw.

I don't know how much straw a camel can carry. I don't know how heavy a burden I can carry. We all have a tendency, however, to suppose that we can carry far less than we actually can.

"MY BURDEN IS LIGHT"

There have been times in my life when I have uttered foolish prayers. When I have been hard pressed, I have cried out to God: "This much and no more, Lord. I can't handle another setback. One more straw and I'm finished." It seems that every time I pray like that God puts a fresh load on my back. It is as if He answers my prayer by saying, "Don't tell *Me* how much you can bear."

God knows our limits far better than we do. In one respect, we are very much like camels. When the camel's load is heavy, he doesn't ask his master for more weight. His knees get a bit wobbly and he groans beneath the burden, but he can take on more before his back will break. The promise of God is not that He will never give us more weight than we *want* to carry. The promise of God is that He will never put more on us than we *can* bear.

Note that Paul did not say, "We are *lightly* pressed on every side." He said that we are *hard* pressed. At first glance, these words seem in direct conflict with the promises of Christ. Jesus said: "Come to Me, all you who labor and are heavy laden, and I will give you rest. Take My yoke upon you and learn from Me, for I am gentle and lowly in heart, and you will find rest for your souls. For My yoke is easy and My burden is light" (Matt. 11:28-30).

It does not always seem to me that the burden Christ gives us is light. With these words, it almost seems as if Jesus approaches us under false pretenses. But His words are true. He *does* give rest to those who are heavy laden. The words *easy* and *light* are relative terms. *Easy* is relative to a standard of difficulty. *Light* is relative to a standard of heaviness. What is difficult to bear without Christ is made far more bearable with Christ. What is a heavy burden to carry alone becomes a far lighter burden to carry with His help.

It is precisely the presence and help of Christ in times of suffering that makes it possible for us to stand up under pressure. It was because of Christ that Paul could triumphantly declare that though he was hard pressed, he was not crushed. We may feel like junked automobiles in a metal compactor, but Christ stands as a shield to prevent the pressure that comes upon us from crushing us entirely.

To suffer without Christ is to risk being totally and completely crushed. I've often wondered how people cope with the trials of life without the strength found in Him. His presence and comfort are so vital that I'm not surprised when unbelievers accuse Christians of using religion as a crutch. We remember Karl Marx's charge that "religion is the opiate of the people." He was referring to opium, a narcotic used for dulling the effects of pain. Others have charged that religion is a bromide used by the weak in times of trouble.

Several years ago, I had knee surgery. During my recuperation, I used crutches. I used them because I needed them. Likewise, years earlier I was in the hospital for another operation. After surgery, I was given painkilling drugs every four hours. I recall watching the clock during the fourth hour, eagerly awaiting the moment when I could push the call button for the nurse to get another dose. I was grateful for the painkillers, just as I was grateful for my crutches years later.

I am far more grateful for Christ. It is no shame to call on Him for help in times of trouble. It is His delight to minister to us in our time of pain. There is no scandal in the mercy of God to the afflicted. He is like a Father who pities His children and moves to comfort them when they are hurting. To suffer without the comfort of God is no virtue. To lean upon His comfort is no vice, contrary to Marx.

SURPRISED BY SUFFERING

Paul added, "We are perplexed, but not in despair." Perplexity often accompanies suffering. When we are stricken with illness or grief, we are often bewildered and confused. Our first question is "Why?" We ask, "How could God allow this to happen to me?"

I remember the story of a distraught father who was deeply grieved by the death of his son. He went to see his pastor, and in his bewildered anger he asked, "Where was God when my son died?" The pastor replied with a calm spirit, "The same place He was when *His* Son died."

There is an element of surprise connected to suffering. We learn early that pain is a part of life, but the learning process is usually gradual. I am amused by the way my three-year-old grandson handles pain. When something hurts him, he declares, "Pap-pap, I have an 'ouch.'" He uses the word *ouch* as a noun. If his "ouch" is slight, a simple kiss will make it disappear. If it is more severe, he asks for an "andbaid."

Most childhood illnesses and bruises are minor. When a child gets a stomach virus, he usually doesn't worry about cancer. He learns quickly that the discomfort of a childhood illness is soon over. As adults, however, we move into another level of disease and pain. Though we move through stages of preparation, we are never quite ready when we are afflicted with a more serious illness.

I remember my daughter's first visit to the hospital. She was six years old and had to have her tonsils removed. As parents, we went through all the steps of preparing her and shielding her from what was coming. We read her the children's books about going to the hospital. We assured her that after the operation she would be allowed the treat of her favorite ice cream.

The trip to the hospital was an adventure. The pediatric wing of the hospital was brightly decorated. The nurses entertained our daughter and her roommate with toys. Her spirits were high and apprehension was at a minimum.

When the girls were taken into surgery, we awaited their return from the recovery room. I will never forget the vision of my daughter when she looked at me after she had awakened. She was a pitiful sight. Dried blood was crusted at the edge of her lips. Her face was ashen. But what was most haunting was her look of fear, shock, and betrayal. She was experiencing a new threshold of pain. It was as if she was saying to me with her eyes: "How could you? You knew it would be like this and you lied to me." The last thing she cared about at that moment was ice cream. She was surprised by her pain, for it was not what she expected.

I am sure my daughter had the same questions about me as we do about our heavenly Father when sudden pain is thrust upon us. Like my daughter, we are often surprised that God allows such deep affliction to befall us. The surprise stems not so much from what God leads us to believe but from what we hear from misguided teachers. The zealous person who promises us a life free from suffering has found his message from a source other than Scripture.

In fact, Scripture admonishes us *not* to think that it is a strange or unusual thing that we should suffer. Peter wrote: "Beloved, do not think it strange concerning the fiery trial which is to try you, as though some strange thing happened to you; but rejoice to the extent that you partake of Christ's sufferings, that when His glory is revealed, you may also be glad with exceeding joy" (1 Peter 4:12–13). These words echo Paul's statement about "filling up what is lacking" in the sufferings of Christ (Col. 1:24), a curious affirmation that we will look at more closely in the next chapter.

Peter adds these words: "But let none of you suffer as a murderer, a thief, an evildoer, or as a busybody in other people's matters. Yet if anyone suffers as a Christian, let him not be ashamed, but let him glorify God in this matter" (1 Peter 4:15–16). When the criminal suffers for his crime, he may be distressed, but he has no reason to be perplexed. There is no surprise that punishment should be the consequence of crime. There is shame attached to this sort of suffering.

To suffer as a Christian carries no shame. Peter concludes: "Therefore let those who suffer according to the will of God commit their souls to Him in doing good, as to a faithful Creator" (1 Peter 4:19). Here, Peter erases all doubt about the question of whether it is ever the will of God that we should suffer. He speaks of those who suffer "according to the will of God." This text means that suffering itself is part of the sovereign will of God.

Earlier in his epistle, Peter spoke of the fruit of our suffering:

> In this you greatly rejoice, though now for a little while, if need be, you have been grieved by various trials, that the genuineness of your faith, being much more precious than gold that perishes, though it is tested by fire, may be found to praise, honor, and glory at the revelation of Jesus Christ, whom having not seen you love. Though now you do not see Him, yet believing, you rejoice with joy inexpressible and full of glory, receiving the end of your faith—the salvation of your souls. (1 Peter 1:6–9)

This passage shows how it is possible to be perplexed but not in despair. Our suffering has a purpose—it helps us toward the end of our faith, which is the salvation of our souls. Suffering is a crucible. As gold is refined in the fire, purged of its dross and impurities, so our faith is tested by fire. Gold perishes. Our souls do not. We experience pain and grief for a season. It is while we are in the fire that perplexity assails us. But there is another side to the fire. As the dross burns away, the genuineness of faith is purified unto the salvation of our souls.

DESPAIR AND THE DESIRE TO DIE

It is when we view our suffering as meaningless—without purpose—that we are tempted to despair. A woman who endures the travail of childbirth is able to do it because she knows that the end result will be a new life. But not all of those who are terminally ill have the same hope of a good result as those giving birth to a child. If death is the end, the suffering that attends it *should* drive us to full and final despair.

However, the message of Christ is that death is not unto death but unto life. So the analogy of childbirth applies. In fact, it is used to describe the suffering of Christ and of the whole creation. Isaiah wrote, "He shall see the labor of his soul and be satisfied" (Isa. 53:11). Likewise, Paul told us: "For we know that the whole creation groans and labors with birth pangs together until now. Not only that, but we also who have the firstfruits of the Spirit, even we ourselves groan within ourselves, eagerly waiting for the adoption, the redemption of our body" (Rom. 8:22–23).

We may be perplexed, but we should not despair. The pain of suffering in itself would be enough to drive us to despair were we not persuaded of the redemption that lies before us.

Still, even that redemption is not always enough to keep us from approaching the rim of despair. Scripture repeatedly reveals the struggles of the greatest saints with the problem of despair. More than one biblical figure cursed the day of his birth and pleaded for the privilege of death.

Moses faced the dark night of the soul when he cried out to God: "If You treat me like this, please kill me here and now—if I have found favor in Your sight—and do not let me see my wretchedness!" (Num. 11:15). Job cursed the day of his birth, saying: "Why did I not die at birth? Why did I not perish when I came from the womb? Why did the knees receive me? Or why the breasts, that I should nurse? For now I would have lain still and been quiet, I would have been asleep; then I would have been at rest" (Job 3:11–13). Jeremiah expressed the same sentiment: "Cursed be the day in which I was born! Let the day not be blessed in which my mother bore me! Let the man be cursed who brought news to my father, saying, "A male child has been born to you!" making him very glad. . . . Why did I come forth from the womb to see labor and sorrow, that my days should be consumed with shame?" (Jer. 20:14–15, 18).

It is when suffering lingers that we are pushed to these depths. The Danish philosopher Søren Kierkegaard once remarked that one of the worst states a human being can face is to want to die and not be allowed to do so. I have personally encountered people in this condition. Many elderly people have said to me: "I wish the Lord would take me. Why does He make me linger?"

DEATH WITH DIGNITY?

The deep desire to be released from suffering lies at the core of the issue of euthanasia. It is argued that we are more humane to animals than we are to people. We shoot horses and we put our dogs to sleep, but we maintain human life as long as possible.

Historically, both the church and the medical profession (following the Hippocratic Oath) have followed the maxim that we ought to do everything possible to sustain life. But with the advent of modern techniques, it is now possible to keep people technically alive beyond the scope of any possible hope for recovery. Thus, modern technology has introduced severe moral dilemmas into the matter of dying.

It must be said that God does not permit us to commit suicide. Suicide, in its fullest expression, involves a surrender to despair. (This does not mean that suicide is the unpardonable sin. People commit suicide for all sorts of reasons and in all sorts of conditions. We don't really know the state of mind people are in when they do it. We leave the question of the fate of suicide victims to the mercy of God.) Whatever the complexities of suffering, we know that we are not given suicide as an option for death.

In the debate over euthanasia, distinctions are made between *active* and *passive* euthanasia. Active euthanasia involves taking direct steps to kill a suffering person. This includes such procedures as lethal injection. Simply stated, passive euthanasia involves the cessation of the use of extraordinary life-support methods. Passive euthanasia is sometimes known as "pulling the plug" or "allowing nature to take its course." Here the issue of dying with dignity becomes paramount.

I once was asked to address a convocation of eight hundred physicians on the issue of "pulling the plug." The doctors were acutely aware of the problems. How should the plug be pulled? Who should pull the plug? When should the plug be pulled?

When we consider the various means by which life can be artificially sustained, it becomes clear that there are many ways to "pull the plug."

IV tubes can be removed, allowing a person to starve to death. Respirators can be turned off. Medication can be stopped. When these steps are taken, the line between so-called active and passive euthanasia quickly becomes blurred. Likewise, the difference between *ordinary* and *extraordinary* means of life support is not always clear. Yesterday's extraordinary means becomes today's ordinary means.

The problem is complicated by the question of *who* makes the decision. The doctor doesn't want to play God. The family can be crushed by guilt surrounding the decision. No pastor feels adequate to the task, and it is terrifying to leave the issue in the hands of the legal community. Yet decisions in these matters have to be made daily in hospitals all over the world. Not to make a decision is to make a decision.

I don't have all the answers to this dilemma, but I am sure of two things. The first is that the issues must be decided in light of the overarching principle of the sanctity of human life. We must bend over backward to insure the maintenance of human life. If we err, it is better to err in favor of life rather than to cheapen it in any way. Second, the decision must involve three parties at least, perhaps four. It must involve the physicians, the family, the clergy, and when possible, the patient.

This issue is part of the perplexity of suffering. At all costs, the decisions we make must not be made from a point of view of despair. At all times, we must keep the goal of redemption in mind lest hope be swallowed up by despair.

As I noted above, the only way to avoid despair is to place our faith in Jesus Christ for the salvation God provides. David summed up the matter: "I would have lost heart, unless I had believed that I would see the goodness of the LORD in the land of the living" (Ps. 27:13). Likewise, the apostle Paul, in the same epistle in which he said, "We are perplexed, but not in despair," also wrote:

> We do not want you to be ignorant, brethren, of our trouble which came
> to us in Asia; that we were burdened beyond measure, above strength,
> so that we despaired even of life. Yes, we had the sentence of death in

ourselves, that we should not trust in ourselves but in God who raises the dead, who delivered us from so great a death, and does deliver us; in whom we trust that He will still deliver us. (2 Cor. 1:8–10)

Paul entered into despair. But his despair was limited. It was not ultimate despair. He despaired of his earthly life. He was sure that he was going to die. But Paul did not despair of the ultimate deliverance from death. He knew the promise of Christ for victory over death.

CHAPTER TWO

WALKING
THE VIA DOLOROSA

"He began to be sorrowful and deeply distressed."

—Matthew 26:37

S orrow and deep distress marked the inner spirit of Jesus as He entered into prayer in the Garden of Gethsemane. This was a moment of intense agony for Him. He was nearing the climax of His great passion. The great passion of Jesus was the focal point of His divine vocation, His calling. No one was ever called by God to greater suffering than God's only begotten Son.

Our Savior was a suffering Savior. He went before us into the uncharted land of agony and death. He went where no man is called to go. His Father gave Him a cup to drink that will never touch our lips. God will not ask us to endure anything comparable to the distress Christ took on Himself. Wherever God calls us to go, whatever He summons us to endure, will fall far short of what Jesus experienced.

From the beginning of His ministry, Jesus was conscious of His mission. He knew He was under a death sentence. His "disease" was terminal. On the cross, the Father afflicted Him not with one terminal disease but with every terminal disease. Of course, this does not mean that Jesus received a positive biopsy report or that a physician diagnosed Him with advanced leprosy. He went to His death with no outward evidence of any known disease. But the cumulative pain of every disease was laid on Him. He bore in His body the ravages of every evil, every sickness, and every pain known to the human race.

Jesus suffered so deeply because the extent of evil in the world is so vast. Every consequence of every sin of each one of His people was placed on Him. To carry this dreadful burden was His vocation. To bear this pain and disease was His mission. The magnitude of this horror is beyond our understanding. But He understood it because it was His to bear.

Jesus endured His suffering in order to redeem His people. But those He redeemed are not thereby delivered from all pain and misery. Indeed, as we shall see, we His people are called to participate in His suffering.

THE SCANDAL OF A SUFFERING CHRIST

The idea that the Son of God would come in the flesh and suffer was unthinkable to many of His contemporaries. The scandalous news of the New Testament is that God became incarnate. The eternal, divine Word was made flesh. His flesh was vulnerable to all physical torment.

The Greeks' idea of God was so spiritual, so ethereal, that they did not even have room for the concept of incarnation. In their view, God could never be involved with physical suffering simply because God could never be involved with anything physical.

The Jews could accept the idea that God could appear in human form, but that God in human flesh could actually suffer was beyond their comprehension.

Following the moment of Peter's greatest confession at Caesarea Philippi came one of the sharpest rebukes he ever heard from Jesus. It all began with

Peter's answer to Jesus' question, "Who do you say that I am?" (Matt. 16:15). Peter replied, "You are the Christ, the Son of the living God" (16:16).

For this response Peter received the benediction of Jesus: "Blessed are you, Simon Bar-Jonah, for flesh and blood has not revealed this to you, but my Father who is in heaven. And I also say to you that you are Peter, and on this rock I will build My church, and the gates of Hades shall not prevail against it" (16:17–18). What higher commendation could a man receive than this blessing from Christ Himself?

Moments later, however, this same man received a stinging rebuke from Jesus: "Get behind Me, Satan! You are an offense to Me, for you are not mindful of the things of God, but the things of men" (16:23).

These words were spoken not to Satan but to Peter. The dialogue here is volatile. One moment Jesus put His benediction on Peter and the next moment He called him "Satan." How can we explain this dramatic shift in tone and words? Jesus was not given to undue severity in His treatment of people. Neither was He two-faced, praising with one side of His mouth and cursing with the other.

This shift of speech must be understood in light of the interval that passed between the commendation and the rebuke. The interval contained an exchange between Peter and Jesus regarding suffering: "From that time Jesus began to show to His disciples that He must go to Jerusalem, and suffer many things from the elders and chief priests and scribes, and be killed, and be raised again the third day" (16:21).

We notice here that Jesus was showing that He must suffer and die. His trip to Jerusalem was not optional. He had a destiny to fulfill, a rendezvous on Golgotha. This "mustness" was rooted in His vocation. He was called to perform a task. It was His duty to suffer and die.

It was precisely at this point of duty that Peter challenged Him: "Then Peter took Him aside and began to rebuke Him, saying, 'Far be it from You, Lord; this shall not happen to you!'" (16:22).

At least Peter had the grace to rebuke his Lord privately. He didn't flaunt his arrogance publicly, though the Holy Spirit entered his unspeakable presumption in the public record of Scripture.

Peter demanded that Jesus distance Himself from suffering and death. He wanted a Savior unsullied by suffering. He wanted the kingdom to come Satan's way rather than God's way. God's way was the way of the cross, the *Via Dolorosa*. Jesus recognized in Peter's demand the same seductive suggestion that Satan had offered in the wilderness.

Theologians argue about when in Jesus' life it entered His consciousness that He must suffer and die, but the Bible makes it clear that the idea of the suffering Messiah was formulated long before Caesarea Philippi. The concept was foreshadowed as early as Genesis 3:15: "And I will put enmity between you and the woman, and between your seed and her Seed; He shall bruise your head, and you shall bruise His heel." This is the *Protevangelium*, the first hint of the gospel that was to come. Later, the idea was greatly expanded in the Suffering Servant motif of Isaiah.

Furthermore, the suffering of Jesus was prophesied to Mary by the venerable Simeon in the temple: "Behold, this Child is destined for the fall and rising of many in Israel, and for a sign which will be spoken against (yes, a sword will pierce through your own soul also), that the thoughts of many hearts may be revealed" (Luke 2:34–35). This passage makes it clear that His mother received a foreshadowing of a piercing sword in the first weeks of His life.

At age twelve, Jesus declared that He *must* be about His Father's business (Luke 2:49). By then He was aware of a *mustness*, a duty that was His to perform. Whether He realized the full import of that duty at such an early age is a matter of conjecture. But certainly by the time He arrived at the Garden of Gethsemane there was no longer any question.

In the garden, He entered into His sorrow. He said to His disciples: "My soul is exceedingly sorrowful, even to death. Stay here and watch with Me" (Matt. 26:38).

The Scriptures tell us that after saying these words, Jesus went farther into the olive grove and fell on His face as He prayed: "O My Father, if it is possible, let this cup pass from Me; nevertheless, not as I will, but as You will" (Matt. 26:39). Luke adds to the historical record these words: "And being in agony, He prayed more earnestly. Then His sweat became like great drops of blood falling down to the ground" (Luke 22:44).

ACCEPTING NO AS GOD'S WILL

I am astonished that, in the light of the clear biblical record, anyone would have the audacity to suggest that it is wrong for the afflicted in body or soul to couch their prayers for deliverance in terms of "If it be thy will. . . ." We are told that when affliction comes, God always wills healing, that He has nothing to do with suffering, and that all we must do is claim the answer we seek by faith. We are exhorted to claim God's yes before He speaks it.

Away with such distortions of biblical faith! They are conceived in the mind of the Tempter, who would seduce us into exchanging faith for magic. No amount of pious verbiage can transform such falsehood into sound doctrine. We must accept the fact that God sometimes says no. Sometimes He calls us to suffer and die even if we want to claim the contrary.

Never did a man pray more earnestly than Christ prayed in Gethsemane. Who will charge Jesus with failure to pray in faith? He put His request before the Father with sweat like blood: "Take this cup away from me." This prayer was straightforward and without ambiguity—Jesus was crying out for relief. He asked for the horribly bitter cup to be removed. Every ounce of His humanity shrank from the cup. He begged the Father to relieve Him of His duty.

But God said no. The way of suffering was the Father's plan. It was the Father's will. The cross was not Satan's idea. The passion of Christ was not the result of human contingency. It was not the accidental contrivance of Caiaphas, Herod, or Pilate. The cup was prepared, delivered, and administered by almighty God.

Jesus qualified His prayer: "If it is Your will. . . ." Jesus did not "name it and claim it." He knew His Father well enough to understand that it might not be His will to remove the cup. So the story does not end with the words, "And the Father repented of the evil He had planned, removed the cup, and Jesus lived happily ever after." Such words border on blasphemy. The gospel is not a fairy tale. The Father would not negotiate the cup. Jesus was called to drink it to its last dregs. And He accepted it. "Nevertheless, not My will, but Yours, be done" (Luke 22:42).

This "nevertheless" was the supreme prayer of faith. The prayer of faith is not a demand that we place on God. It is not a presumption of a granted request. The authentic prayer of faith is one that models Jesus' prayer. It is always uttered in a spirit of subordination. In all our prayers, we must let God be God. No one tells the Father what to do, not even the Son. Prayers are always to be requests made in humility and submission to the Father's will.

The prayer of faith is a prayer of trust. The very essence of faith is trust. We trust that God knows what is best. The spirit of trust includes a willingness to do what the Father wants us to do. Christ embodied that kind of trust in Gethsemane.

Though the text is not explicit, it is clear that Jesus left the garden with the Father's answer to His plea. There was no cursing or bitterness. His meat and His drink were to do the Father's will. Once the Father said no, it was settled. Jesus prepared Himself for the cross.

REDEEMING THROUGH SUFFERING

In the life and passion of Christ, we see most clearly that suffering is the way God has chosen to bring redemption to a fallen world. Jesus was known as a man of sorrows, one who was acquainted with grief (Isa. 53:3). His life and ministry followed in detail the mission of the Suffering Servant of the Lord set forth by the prophet Isaiah.

We read a fascinating story in the book of Acts:

> Now an angel of the Lord spoke to Philip, saying, "Arise and go toward the south along the road which goes down from Jerusalem to Gaza." This is desert. So he arose and went. And behold, a man of Ethiopia, a eunuch of great authority under Candace the queen of the Ethiopians, who had charge of all her treasury, and had come to Jerusalem to worship, was returning. And sitting in his chariot, he was reading Isaiah the prophet. Then the Spirit said to Philip, "Go near and overtake this chariot."

So Philip ran to him, and heard him reading the prophet Isaiah, and said, "Do you understand what you are reading?"

And he said, "How can I, unless someone guides me?" And he asked Philip to come up and sit with him. The place in the Scripture which he read was this:

"He was led as a sheep to the slaughter;
And as a lamb before its shearer is silent,
So He opened not His mouth.
In His humiliation His justice was taken away,
And who will declare His generation?
For His life is taken from the earth."

So the eunuch answered Philip and said, "I ask you, of whom does the prophet say this, of himself or of some other man?" Then Philip opened his mouth, and beginning at this Scripture, preached Jesus to him. (Acts 8:26–35)

The Ethiopian eunuch asked Philip a crucial question. He had been reading from Isaiah 53 and was puzzled. He asked, "Of whom does the prophet say this, of himself or of some other man?" He wanted to know who was the Suffering Servant of the Lord.

Philip's answer was directly to the point. Isaiah, he told the Ethiopian, was talking about Jesus.

The fact that the New Testament identifies Jesus with the Suffering Servant of Israel may seem so obvious that you may wonder why I take time to expand upon it. But it matters profoundly. In the first place, our understanding of Jesus is tied to this question. I do not think it is an overstatement to declare that the New Testament portrait of Jesus stands or falls with this issue. However, the agonizing question of the meaning of our own suffering is tied to it, as well.

In modern times, we have seen a kind of biblical scholarship that considers all references by Jesus to Isaiah's Suffering Servant prophecies as inventions of the New Testament writers. In a word, the biblical writers allegedly "doctored" the history of Jesus. The theory holds that after Jesus went through His passion, the leaders of the early church had to invent an explanation for all this suffering. Therefore, they created this link between Isaiah's Suffering Servant and Jesus. Then they put words into Jesus' mouth that He never uttered.

The critics have an ax to grind against the biblical view of Christ. Their ax is so heavy that they bump themselves in the head with it. If we know anything of the historical Jesus, we know Him as one who suffered and died as the Servant of God.

Luke's Gospel records these words of Jesus: "For I say to you that this which is written must still be accomplished in Me: 'And He was numbered with the transgressors.' For the things concerning me have an end" (Luke 22:37).

Here Jesus quoted directly from Isaiah 53. He identified Himself with the Suffering Servant of God. The nation of Israel was called to be a suffering servant. That vocation was then personalized and crystallized in one man, who represented Israel. Philip's answer was clear: that man was Jesus.

PARTICIPATING IN HIS SUFFERING

Jesus suffered for us. Yet we are called to participate in His suffering. Though He was uniquely the fulfillment of Isaiah's prophecy, there is still an application of this vocation for us. We are given both the duty and the privilege to participate in the suffering of Christ.

A mysterious reference to this idea is found in the writings of the apostle Paul: "I now rejoice in my sufferings for you, and fill up in my flesh what is lacking in the afflictions of Christ, for the sake of His body, which is the church" (Col. 1:24). Here Paul declared that he rejoiced in his suffering. Surely he did not mean that he enjoyed pain and affliction. Rather, the cause of his joy was found in the meaning of his suffering. He said that he filled up "what is lacking in the afflictions of Christ."

On the surface, Paul's explanation is astonishing. What could possibly have been lacking in the afflictions of Christ? Did Christ only half-finish His redemptive work, leaving it to Paul to complete it? Was Jesus overstating the case when He cried from the cross, "It is finished"? What exactly was lacking in the suffering of Christ?

In terms of the *value* of Jesus' suffering, it is blasphemous to suggest anything was lacking. The merit of His atoning sacrifice is infinite. Nothing could possibly be added to His perfect obedience to make it even more perfect. Nothing can be more perfect than perfect. What is absolutely perfect cannot be augmented.

The merit of Jesus' suffering is sufficient to atone for every sin that has ever been or ever will be committed. His once-for-all atoning death needs no repetition (Heb. 10:10). Old Testament sacrifices were repeated precisely because they were imperfect shadows of the reality that was to come (Heb. 10:1).

It was not by accident that the Roman Catholic Church appealed to Paul's words in Colossians 1:24 to support its concept of the treasury of merits, by which the merits of the saints are supposedly added to the merit of Christ to cover the deficiencies of sinners. This doctrine was at the eye of the Protestant Reformation tornado. It was this eclipse of the sufficiency and perfection of Christ's suffering that was at the heart of Martin Luther's protest.

Though we vigorously deny Rome's interpretation of this passage, we are still left with our question. If Paul's suffering did not add merit to what was lacking in Christ's sufferings, what did it add?

The answer to this difficult question lies in the broader teaching of the New Testament in regard to the believer's call to participate in the humiliation of Christ. Our baptism signifies that we are buried with Christ. Paul repeatedly pointed out that unless we are willing to participate in the humiliation of Jesus, we will not participate in His exaltation (see 2 Timothy 2:11–12).

Paul rejoiced that his suffering was a benefit to the church. The church is called to imitate Christ. It is called to walk the *Via Dolorosa*. Paul's favorite metaphor for the church was the image of the human body. The church is called the body of Christ. In one sense, it is proper to call the church the "continuing incarnation." The church is really the mystical body of Christ on earth.

Christ so linked His church to Himself that when He first called Paul on the Damascus Road He said, "Saul, Saul, why do you persecute *Me?*" (Acts 9:4, emphasis added). Saul was not literally persecuting Jesus. Jesus had already ascended to heaven. He was already out of reach of Saul's hostility. Saul was busy persecuting Christians. But Jesus felt such solidarity with His church that He regarded an attack upon His body, the church, as a personal attack on Himself.

The church is not Christ. Christ is perfect; the church is imperfect. Christ is the Redeemer; the church is the company of the redeemed. However, the church belongs to Christ. The church is redeemed by Christ. The church is the bride of Christ. The church is indwelt by Christ.

In light of this solidarity, the church participates in Christ's suffering. But this participation adds nothing to Christ's merit. The sufferings of Christians may benefit other people, but they always fall short of atonement. I cannot atone for anyone's sins, not even for my own. Yet my suffering may be of great benefit to other people. It may also serve as a witness to the One whose sufferings *were* an atonement.

The word for "witness" in the New Testament, *martus*, is the source of the English word *martyr*. Those who suffered and died for the cause of Christ were called martyrs because by their suffering they bore witness to Christ.

What is lacking in the afflictions of Jesus is the ongoing suffering that God calls His people to endure. God calls people of every generation to suffer. Again, this suffering is not to fulfill any deficiency in the merit of Christ, but to fulfill our destinies as witnesses to the perfect Suffering Servant of God.

What does this mean in practical terms? My father suffered a series of cerebral hemorrhages that caused him great suffering and eventually ended his life. I'm sure that while he was suffering he must have asked God, "Why?" On the surface, his suffering seemed useless. It seemed as though his pain was for no good reason.

I must be very careful. I do not think that my father's suffering was in any way an atonement for my sins. Neither do I think I can read God's mind with respect to the ultimate reason for my father's suffering. But I know this:

my father's suffering made a profound impact on my life. It was through my father's death that I was brought to Christ. I am not saying that the ultimate reason my father was called to suffer and die was so that I could become a Christian. I don't know the sovereign purpose of God in it. But I do know that God *used* that suffering in a redemptive way for me. My dad's suffering drove me into the arms of the Suffering Savior.

We are followers of Christ. We follow Him to the Garden of Gethsemane. We follow Him into the hall of judgment. We follow Him along the *Via Dolorosa*. We follow Him unto death. But the gospel declares that we also follow Him through the gates of heaven. Because we suffer with Him, we also shall be raised with Him. If we are humiliated with Him, we also shall be exalted with Him.

Because of Christ, our suffering is not useless. It is part of the total plan of God, who has chosen to redeem the world through the pathway of suffering.

CHAPTER THREE

A CASE STUDY IN SUFFERING

The vice president of operations of a large corporation became intensely jealous of a district manager in the company. The district manager enjoyed a close personal relationship with the chairman of the board. Moved by his jealousy, the vice president lodged a complaint with the chairman.

"I think we ought to get rid of Joe Hawkins," he suggested.

"Why?" the chairman asked. "He's one of our most productive managers. I think he's doing an outstanding job. And besides, he is the most loyal employee we have."

"Loyal? You think he's loyal?" the vice president said with dripping cynicism. "He's only loyal because you pay him such a high salary. You give him benefits that no one else receives. Besides, you've built a wall of protection around him. Everybody knows that he's your fair-haired boy. I wonder how loyal he'd be if you put the heat on him. Cut his salary and benefits, then see how loyal he is."

The chairman was irritated by this suggestion, but he responded to the challenge. "All right," he said. "Let's see about it. Go ahead and cut his salary. Put some heat on. I think you'll see that Hawkins will maintain his loyalty."

The vice president gave a sarcastic laugh. "You just let me at him and he'll betray you and the company in a minute."

The vice president left the boardroom and put together a scheme to bring Joe crashing down. First, he cut his salary in half and cancelled his health insurance. Then he approached some of Joe's coworkers and enlisted them in his scheme. They were eager to join in. They gleefully contrived plans of industrial sabotage to destroy Joe's productivity record. They falsified reports and covertly disrupted some of the machinery in the plant. Suddenly, Joe's plant was besieged with customer complaints about poor quality.

The heat was on, but Joe took it in stride. He worked hard to solve the mysterious rash of problems that had arisen. This merely fueled the antagonism of his enemies. They began to put more pressure on. "Accidents" began to happen in the plant. The conspirators even started to harass Joe's family. To make matters worse, Joe suddenly became ill. The vice president had bribed a corrupt physician to introduce a virulent strain of bacteria into Joe's food.

Joe's world began to fall apart. His sickness took its toll. Coupled with the plunging productivity of his plant, his star began to fade.

Some of his closest friends came to him with sharp criticism. "What's wrong with you, Hawkins?" they asked. "You've lost something. Your performance is down. No wonder they cut your salary."

Joe's friends began to think that their former opinion of him had been wrong. They assumed that Joe must have done something really bad for his life to have taken such a sudden and drastic turn for the worse. One of his friends even came to him with "spiritual" counsel. "Joe," he said, "I need to tell you something in love. The troubles you've been having must come from God. I think it is all a kind of punishment for unconfessed sin in your life. Maybe if you repent, things will start to go better for you."

"Maybe you're right," Joe replied. "I'm not aware of anything I've done to deserve this, but I will certainly search my soul about it."

"But the chairman cut your salary in half. Doesn't that tell you something?"

"Well, the chairman has a right to do that. He's always been fair with me. I'm sure he knows what he is doing. He must have a good reason for his action," Joe answered.

Then Joe's wife got into the act. "Honey," she said one evening, "I think it's time for you to resign. Your health is failing and the company is treating you like dirt. After all your years of faithful service, this is the thanks you get. Let's get out and start over somewhere else. You're crazy to keep working for a company like this."

"No, Hon," Joe answered. "I can't leave."

"Why not?" his wife demanded.

"I owe it to the chairman of the board to stay on."

"Are you crazy? You don't owe him anything. You've given him the best years of your life, and now this. He owes *you*! You don't owe him a thing. Why don't you face it, Joe, the chairman's as rotten as the deal he's given you."

"No!" Joe snapped in anger. "I just can't believe that he would treat me unfairly on purpose."

"Then you'd better talk to him face to face. I'd love to hear what he says when you confront him."

"OK, OK, I'll talk to him," Joe promised.

The next day, Joe made an appointment to see the chairman. When he was ushered into the teak-paneled office, the chairman greeted him in a friendly manner. "Hi, Joe. What can I do for you?"

Joe got straight to the point. He gushed out his grievances in a torrent of rage. "What's going on here?" he demanded. "You've cut my salary in half. You stand by and let a bunch of thieves sabotage my plant. You've taken away my health benefits. What did I do to deserve this kind of treatment? I've been loyal to you and to the company for years, and now you treat me like this! Who do you think you are, anyway?"

The chairman listened patiently to Joe's diatribe. Then he responded. "Let me ask you some questions, Joe," he said. "Do you own this company?"

"No, sir," Joe replied.

"Did you build this place from scratch? Did you risk your own capital in this operation? Do you make payroll twice a month? Are you the chairman of the board?"

To all these questions, Joe shook his head.

"Tell me, Joe, who are you to tell me how to run my company? I've given you everything I ever promised you and more. Look at your contract. Does your contract specify that you should receive all the bonuses I've given you over the years?"

Again Joe had to give an honest answer. "No, sir, you really have been more than kind to me."

"You say I've been more than kind. Do you think I've changed? Do you think I'm not aware of what's been going on recently? I know exactly what's going on in your plant. I've been following the matter closely. Nothing has escaped my notice.

"Joe, I'm going to ask you to do something for me. You've trusted me in the past. Trust me now. I guarantee you that I will straighten things out. I have a plan. Those who have plotted against you will get everything they deserve. Do you really think I would let them get away with this?"

Joe felt awful. He began to stammer an apology. "I'm sorry," he said. "I had no right to come in here and lay all these accusations on you. I've complained once, but no more. You'll never hear another word of protest out of my mouth. Do whatever you will. I trust you."

The chairman smiled. Then he spoke into the intercom to his secretary. "Ms. Franklin," he said, "have the vice president of operations report to my office immediately."

"Don't leave yet, Joe. I have a few final words for you. First, I want you to know that when the vice president of operations gets here, I'm going to give him his walking papers. Beginning tomorrow morning, you will be the vice president of operations. You will receive double the salary you had before your pay was cut. I'm restoring your health benefits. And I have located a specialist who can treat and cure your disease.

"You have been loyal to me, Joe, more loyal than any other employee. You've endured a lot without cursing me behind my back. Now it is time for you to be vindicated."

"I knew it," Joe exclaimed. "I had my moments of doubt, but deep down inside I knew you would fix everything. Now I really feel embarrassed for all those accusations I made to you. How can you ever forgive me?"

"Joe, don't worry about it. That's one thing I know how to do—forgive. I major in forgiveness."

ARE SIN AND SUFFERING CONNECTED?

By now you probably have recognized that this is the story of the biblical character Job, thinly disguised in modern terminology. The story of Job is a case study in human suffering. It chronicles the drama of a righteous man who underwent extreme misery in this world. His misery was compounded by his friends' insensitivity toward him. They made an assumption that the Bible forbids. They assumed that Job's degree of suffering was in direct proportion to his sin. They assumed that there is a ratio in our lives between suffering and guilt. Since Job's suffering was great, it must have been a sign that his sin was equally great.

God does not allow this equation. We remember the question put to Jesus about the man who was born blind: "Now as Jesus passed by, He saw a man who was blind from birth. And His disciples asked Him, saying, 'Rabbi, who sinned, this man or his parents, that he was born blind?' Jesus answered, 'Neither this man nor his parents sinned, but that the works of God should be revealed in him'" (John 9:1–3).

In the science of logic, there is an informal fallacy called the fallacy of the false dilemma. Sometimes it is called the either/or fallacy. This error of reasoning occurs when a problem is presented as if there are only two possible explanations, when in reality there are three or more options.

Some issues are indeed of an either/or character. For example, either there is a God or there is not. There is no third option. But because *some* questions may be reduced to only two alternatives does not mean that *all* questions may be so reduced. This is the error the disciples made concerning the man born blind.

When the disciples considered the plight of the blind man, they assumed there were only two possible explanations for it. Either the blindness was the result of the man's sin or the result of his parents' sin.

Their thinking was wrong, but it was not utterly groundless. They were correct in one assumption. They knew enough about Scripture to realize that there is a connection between suffering and sin. They understood that suffering and death entered the world because of sin. Before sin entered the world, there was no suffering or death.

Death is unnatural. It may be natural to fallen man, but it was not natural to man as he was created. Man was not created to die. He was created with the possibility of death, but not with the necessity of death. Death was introduced as a consequence of sin. If there had been no sin, there would be no death. But when sin entered, the curse of the fall was added. All suffering and death flow out of the complex of sin.

The disciples were partially correct at another point. They were aware that sometimes there is a direct link between a person's sin and his suffering. For instance, God afflicted Miriam with leprosy as a judgment for her sin against Moses (Num. 12:9–10).

The error of the disciples was in their assumption that there is *always* a direct correlation, a fixed ratio, between a person's sin and a person's suffering. In this world, some people suffer far less than what they deserve for their sins, while others endure a greater proportion of suffering. This disparity is seen in David's cry, "Lord, how long will the wicked, how long will the wicked triumph?" (Ps. 94:3).

There are times when we suffer innocently at other people's hands. When that occurs, we are victims of injustice. But that injustice happens on a horizontal plane. No one ever suffers injustice on the vertical plane. That is, no one ever suffers unjustly in terms of his or her relationship with God. As long as we bear the guilt of sin, we cannot protest that God is unjust in allowing us to suffer.

If someone wrongfully causes me to suffer, I have every right to plead with God for vindication, even as Job did. Yet at the same time, I must not complain to God that He is at fault in allowing this suffering to befall me. In terms of my relationship to other people, I may be innocent, but in terms of my relationship to God, I am not an innocent victim. It is one thing for me to ask God for justice in my dealings with men. It is another thing for me to demand justice in my relationship with God. No more perilous demand could be uttered than for a sinner to demand justice from God. The worst thing that could possibly befall me is to receive pure justice from God.

"GOD MEANT IT FOR GOOD"

All of these considerations aside, the fact remains that the disciples still committed the fallacy of the false dilemma. They limited the reason for the man's blindness to two possible explanations (the man's sin or his parents' sin) when there was at least one other explanation that they failed to consider.

Jesus punctured the false dilemma by saying, "Neither!" The reason why the man had been born blind was not because of his sin. Neither was it because of his parents' sin. Jesus declared that the man had been born blind so "that the works of God should be revealed in him." The man born blind had been afflicted with blindness for the glory of God.

This startling truth is a crucial teaching for us. It serves as a warning for us not to jump to conclusions about the "why" of our suffering.

God used the man's blindness for His greater glory. In this case, the "evil" of disease and suffering was made serviceable to God. He triumphed over it and brought His glorious plan to pass through it.

Likewise, we remember the dreadful suffering of Joseph at the hands of his brothers. Yet because of their treachery, the plan of God for all of history was brought to pass. At the moment of Joseph's reconciliation with his brothers, he exclaimed, "You meant evil against me; but God meant it for good, in order to bring it about as it is this day, to save many people alive" (Gen. 50:20).

Here we see God working through evil to accomplish salvation. God's working did not make the evil of Joseph's brothers any less evil. In just the same way, Judas' betrayal of Jesus was a wicked act. It brought unjust suffering upon Jesus, even as Joseph was a victim of his brothers' injustice. But over all injustice, all pain, and all suffering stands a sovereign God who works His plan of salvation *over*, *against*, and even *through* evil.

TRUSTING NO MATTER WHAT

What Jesus declared to His disciples about the blind man is clearly displayed in the book of Job. Had the disciples mastered this Old Testament book, perhaps they would not have fallen into the either/or fallacy. They made the same mistake committed by Job's friends.

Job protested the words of his friends. His reply is poignant: "I have heard many such things; Miserable comforters are you all! Shall words of wind have an end? Or what provokes you that you answer? I also could speak as you do, if your soul were in my soul's place. I could heap up words against you, and shake my head at you; but I would strengthen you with my mouth, and the comfort of my lips would relieve your grief" (Job 16:2–5).

Consider the advice Job received from his wife:

And he took for himself a potsherd with which to scrape himself while he sat in the midst of the ashes. Then his wife said to him, "Do you still hold fast to your integrity? Curse God and die!"

But he said to her, "You speak as one of the foolish women speaks. Shall we indeed accept good from God, and shall we not accept adversity?"

In all this Job did not sin with his lips. (Job 2:8–10)

One of the most difficult challenges a person faces in the midst of suffering is to receive well-intentioned counsel to give up the struggle. This counsel usually comes from those who are closest to us and who love us the most. Jesus' best friends tried to talk Him out of going to Jerusalem, as we saw when we considered Peter's rebuke in the previous chapter.

Likewise, Job's wife told him, "Curse God and die!" She encouraged him to compromise his integrity in order to alleviate his pain. She meant well. She obviously had compassion for her husband. She encouraged him to take the easy way out. But her words only served to increase Job's frustration. Job did not understand why God had called him to suffer, but he did understand that God *had* called him to suffer. It was hard enough for him to be faithful to his vocation without his loved ones trying to talk him out of it.

I once visited a large church in Southern California and was given a tour of the grounds. Our tour took us to a statue hewn out of stone by a Scandinavian sculptor. I was overcome by emotion as I stood before this majestic piece of art. It displayed the figure of Job, his body twisted and distorted in agony. The muscular detail was reminiscent of a work by Michelangelo.

As I stared at the figure, I thought of an artistic technique based on the principle of the "fruitful moment," which was articulated by the philosopher Johann Herder. Painters and sculptors do not ply their craft by the use of movie cameras or videotape. Their objects are still, frozen in a single moment of time. The artist's goal is to capture the crystallized essence of his subject by focusing on one fruitful or pregnant moment that tells the larger story. This was why Rembrandt sketched scores of scenes from the lives of biblical characters before he decided on a single frame to paint. This is why Michelangelo depicted David reaching for a stone. This is why Rodin's *Thinker* is poised in deep reflection. This is why the body of Christ is cradled in the arms of His mother in the *Pieta*.

The sculptor who fashioned the image of Job that I saw in the garden of that church caught Job in the fruitful moment—the nadir of his agony. At the base of the sculpture, chiseled in the stone, were these words: "Though He slay me, yet will I trust Him" (Job 13:15).

When I saw these words at the base of the statue, I stood and wept in silence. No more heroic words were ever uttered by mortal man than these words of testimony from the lips of Job.

GOD HIMSELF AS THE ANSWER TO "WHY?"

Job's trust wavered, but it never died. He mourned. He cried. He protested. He questioned. He even cursed the day of his birth. But he clutched tightly to his only possible hope, his trust in God. At times, Job was hanging on by his fingernails. But he hung on. He cursed himself. He rebuked his wife. But he never cursed God.

Job cried out to God for answers to his questions. He desperately wanted to know why he was called to endure so much suffering. Finally God answered him out of the whirlwind. But the answer was not what Job had expected. God refused to grant Job a detailed explanation of His reasons for the affliction. God did not disclose His secret counsel to Job.

Ultimately the only answer God gave to Job was a revelation of Himself. It was as if God said to him, "Job, *I* am your answer." Job was not asked to trust a plan but a person, a personal God who is sovereign, wise, and good. It was as if God said to Job: "Learn who I am. When you know me, you know enough to handle anything."

God was asking Job to exercise an implicit faith. An implicit faith is not blind faith. It is a faith with vision, a vision enlightened by a knowledge of the character of God.

If God never revealed anything about Himself to us and required us to trust Him in this darkness, the requirement would be for blind faith. We would be asked to make a blind leap of faith into the awful abyss of darkness.

But God never requires such foolish leaps. He never calls us to jump into the darkness. On the contrary, He calls us to forsake the darkness and enter into the light. It is the light of His countenance. It is the radiant light of His person, which has no shadow of turning. When we are bathed in the refulgent splendor of the glory of His person, trust is not blind.

When Job declared, "Though He slay me, yet will I trust Him," he was revealing to us that though his knowledge of God was limited, it was still profound. He knew enough about the character of God to know that God was (and always would be) trustworthy. To be trustworthy simply means to be worthy of trust.

God deserves to be trusted. He merits our trust in Him. The more we understand of His perfections, the more we understand how trustworthy He is. That is why the Christian pilgrimage moves from faith to faith, from strength to strength, and from grace to grace. It moves toward a crescendo. Ironically, the progress passes through suffering and tribulation. That is why Paul could write these words: "We also glory in tribulations, knowing that tribulation produces perseverance; and perseverance, character; and character, hope. Now hope does not disappoint, because the love of God has been poured out in our hearts by the Holy Spirit who was given to us" (Rom. 5:3–5).

Here we are told that "hope does not disappoint." Other translations speak of a hope for which we are not ashamed or embarrassed.

Blind hope, like blind faith, will indeed disappoint us. Blind hope gropes aimlessly in the darkness. It stumbles over unseen obstacles. To put all one's hope into a single goal and to have that goal unfulfilled is to be disappointed.

Hope that is blind can be embarrassing. We stick our necks out only to be left in disgrace if our boldness is not vindicated. But the hope that rests in Christ will not lead to embarrassment. The shame will be upon those who put their hope in something else. The hope that fails is the hope that has no power to overcome suffering.

If I hope in anything or anyone less than One who has power over suffering and, ultimately, death, I am doomed to final disappointment. Suffering will drive me to hopelessness. What character I have will disintegrate.

It is the hope of Christ that makes it possible for us to persevere in times of tribulation and distress. We have an anchor for our souls that rests in the One who has gone before us and conquered.

CHAPTER FOUR

PURPOSE
IN SUFFERING

There is a theological undercurrent that runs through the book of Ecclesiastes and breaks through again and again. We see it when Solomon affirms that "To everything there is a season, a time for every purpose under heaven: A time to be born, and a time to die . . ." (Eccl. 3:1–2), but it appears elsewhere, too. Solomon writes: "I know that whatever God does, it shall be forever. Nothing can be added to it, and nothing taken from it" (3:14); "Consider the work of God; for who can make straight what He has made crooked?" (7:13); and "For I considered all this in my heart, so that I could declare it all: that the righteous and the wise and their works are in the hand of God" (9:1). This theological undercurrent, which is found not just in Ecclesiastes but in the whole Old Testament and indeed in all of Scripture, is simply this: God ordains everything according to His purposes. In other words, God is sovereign.

In my experience, I have never met a professing Christian who looked me in the eye and said that he did not believe in the sovereignty of God. We have an intuitive understanding that if God is God, He *must* be sovereign. It is impossible for God not to be sovereign, and any conception of a god that is less than sovereign is an idol and no god at all. So it is easy for believers to say, "I believe in the sovereignty of God," and we all affirm it on the surface.

However, the sovereignty of God is one of the most difficult doctrines to get in one's bloodstream and into the fiber of daily living, so that we really live life believing that God is in fact sovereign and maintain our trust in Him even when it seems that life is spinning out of control.

A great part of the difficulty we face in terms of really accepting this doctrine stems from the presence of suffering in our lives. We say that we believe that God is sovereign, but when we wrestle with events in our lives that are troublesome, bad things that happen to us, tragedies that befall us, we begin to question either the sovereignty of God or the goodness of God. We ask ourselves: "How could a God who is sovereign and good have allowed these things to happen? Didn't He have the power to prevent these things? Didn't He love me enough to spare me from this pain?" Many of the theologies that flourish in our land are designed to sidestep that problem. They seek to absolve God from any responsibility for the tragedies of human life and to turn the ultimate sovereignty over to the human heart.

We have already seen that our suffering is part of the total plan of God and that God can work through evil to accomplish His plan. The fact that God has a plan is indicative that He has a purpose. The fact that He is sovereign is indicative that He is fulfilling that purpose even when He allows suffering to come upon us. As in the case of Job, He may not reveal what His purpose is, but we have good reason to trust Him.

THE WISDOM OF SOLOMON

The seventh chapter of Ecclesiastes gives us some interesting insights on this topic. The beginning of the chapter sounds like a portion of the book of Proverbs in that it contains a series of aphorisms. It begins with these words "A good name is better than precious ointment" (v. 1). The writers of the wisdom literature of the ancient world often compared and contrasted virtues or other abstract things with concrete things. In this case, the comparison is between a good reputation and a precious ointment. We don't usually think in terms of "precious" ointments because ointments are very inexpensive and we can get them at every pharmacy on the street. But in the ancient world, an ointment that relived pain and suffering was very difficult to find or acquire, so it was seen as extremely valuable. But Solomon says a good name is better than precious ointment. It is a very valuable thing.

Then he goes on to say, "And the day of death [is better] than the day of one's birth." This could be taken in a pessimistic way or from a transcendent viewpoint. So often in the Old Testament, we find people who are on the rim of despair cursing the day they were born. In chapter 1, we noted such comments from Job, Moses, and Jeremiah. When a person looks at life from the perspective of this world, sometimes he gets tired of living.

Remember the song "Old Man River"? The words go, "Tote that barge, lift that bale, get a little drunk and you land in jail." The refrain then says, "That ol' man river, he just keeps rollin' along." That is a modern expression of pessimism, one that reaches its crescendo in the line, "I'm tired of livin' but I'm scared of dyin'." That feeling defines the lot of far too many people in this world.

Ecclesiastes affirms that the day of a person's death is better than the day of his birth. That would be true for the pessimist, who can't wait to get it over with—at least if he only passes into oblivion rather than eternal punishment.

However, this sentiment is also true for the optimist, for the Christian. The day of one's birth is a good day for the believer, but the day of death is the greatest day that a Christian can ever experience in this world because that is the day he goes home, the day he walks across the threshold, the day he enters the Father's house. That is the day of ultimate triumph for the Christian in this world, and yet it is a day we fear and a day that we postpone as long as we possibly can because we don't *really* believe that the day of our death is better than the day of our birth.

THE HOUSES OF MIRTH AND MOURNING

In verses 2–4 of Ecclesiastes 7, Solomon gives us a strange contrast: "Better to go to the house of mourning than to go to the house of feasting, for that is the end of all men; and the living will take it to heart. Sorrow is better than laughter, for by a sad countenance the heart is made better. The heart of the wise is in the house of mourning, but the heart of fools is in the house of mirth."

One of my favorite authors of all time is Herman Melville. In my opinion, the greatest novel ever written by an American is Melville's *Moby Dick*. It is a fantastically profound theological book. But in addition to *Moby Dick*, Melville wrote two lesser books that are somewhat significant. One of them, *Billy Budd*, was made into a Hollywood movie. The other, which is titled *Redburn*, deals with a person's struggle to find the truth. In *Redburn*, one of Melville's characters makes this observation: "Not till we know that one grief outweighs ten thousand joys will we become what Christianity is striving to make us."

What was Melville saying here? He was saying the same thing that we read in the book of Ecclesiastes, where Solomon says it is better for us to go to the house of mourning than to go to the house of feasting. The distinction here is one that is common to wisdom literature. It is the contrast between the wise and the fool. We may go to the house of mirth, to a party, where we have fun, kick back, have a good time, and enjoy entertainment. Parties are not all that serious; we don't have to be contemplative in order to enjoy ourselves there. Certainly there is a time to laugh, a time to dance, a time to celebrate—a time to have a party. But how much do we learn in those circumstances? Times of mirth do very little for the good of our souls.

However, when we go to the house of mourning, we go to an environment where our hearts can be equipped with transcendent wisdom. There's a pithy saying that tells us, "God sometimes puts us on our backs to give us a chance to look up." It sometimes seems that it is only when suffering, pain, or grief invades our lives that we begin to be sober and direct our thinking toward the things of God in a significant way. The house of mourning has a way of prompting us to do that.

Certainly Jesus was one who was often in the house of mourning. He was described as "a Man of sorrows and acquainted with grief" (Isa. 53:3). Yet He spoke of His joy (John 15:11). For the Christian, there can be joy in the midst of suffering, joy that transcends the pain of the moment. But we don't really understand the grounds for this joy in the house of mirth. We discover it in the house of mourning. It is in weeping that we learn to contemplate the goodness of God. It is in mourning that we discover the peace of God that passes understanding.

Solomon goes on to say, "Sorrow is better than laughter." He doesn't mean that sorrow is good and laughter is bad. This is a comparison between the good and the better. It is better for us in the long run to experience sorrow than laughter. Why? Solomon gives us the answer: "For by a sad countenance the heart is made better. The heart of the wise is in the house of mourning, the heart of fools is in the house of mirth."

When we reach verse 13 of Ecclesiastes 7, we get a different perspective. Here Solomon writes, "Consider the work of God." Solomon challenges us to not simply observe God's work but to think deeply about it. We can observe His handiwork everywhere we look, but we need to do more than simply look at it—we need to consider it, to evaluate it, to seek its meaning, to arrive at some kind of understanding. We are to observe the work of God that we might come to a better understanding of the character of God and of the nature of God. We have to learn how to think theologically.

Solomon's next statement is a question that grows out of his own observation and consideration of God's work: "For who can make straight what He has made crooked?" This is a verse I quote perhaps more than any other verse in the whole Bible. I often quote it at the golf course when I play with guys that can't hit the ball straight. They ask me, as a minister, to pray for them. "Can't you do something, R. C? I can't hit the ball right, will you please help me?" I say, "The Bible says, 'What God has made crooked, no man can make straight.'" That's a lighthearted use of this verse, but, of course, the truth Solomon is expressing is very profound. It speaks to God's power and authority, His sovereignty.

THE PROVIDENCE OF GOD

Then, in verse 14, Solomon writes: "In the day of prosperity be joyful, but in the day of adversity consider: surely God has appointed the one as well as the other." The idea communicated here may be the best-kept secret of Christendom. It is an idea that really speaks to the matter of the sovereignty of God. This call to consider the work of God is a call to examine not just creation but the work of God in history. This is a call to reflect on the providence of God, because He is the author of all things mirthful *and* all things mournful.

We have a tendency to say: "Oh, my confidence in God is strengthened when things happen to me that are enjoyable, when good things happen to me. My lips want to speak forth thanksgiving and praise to God. Thank you God for this wonderful thing." In other words, we tend to be able to see the hand of divine providence in our lives when we pray earnestly for something and God says yes. But when we want something desperately and pray about it intensely, but God answers no, what happens? We begin to doubt that there even is a God. So the no response from God is negative in our lives, whereas the yes response affirms our faith.

Solomon is saying that if you want to be wise, you must consider both, because God's hand is as sovereign in the no as it is in the yes. God displays His providence as much in suffering as in prosperity. His sovereign rule is manifested in both.

In the aftermath of the terrorist attack on the World Trade Center and the Pentagon on September 11, 2001, I noticed that a number of different words were used to describe those events, words such as *catastrophe* and *calamity*. But the word I heard perhaps more than any other was *tragedy*. Usually, however, there was an adjective attached to this word to describe the attack. It was called a *senseless* tragedy.

If I had the time to go into a technical, comprehensive analysis of these two words in conjunction with each other, I could demonstrate that the phrase "senseless tragedy" is an oxymoron. For something to be defined in the final analysis as being "tragic," there has to be some standard of good.

The word *tragedy* presupposes some kind of order of purpose in the world. If things can happen in a way that is senseless, there can be no such thing as a tragedy—or a blessing. Everything is simply a meaningless event.

The idea of a "senseless tragedy" represents a worldview that is completely incompatible with Christian thought, because it assumes that something happens without a purpose or a meaning. But if God is God and if God is a God of providence and if God is sovereign, then nothing ever happens that is senseless in the final analysis.

The question that troubles us in reference to the September 11 attacks is, "Why did this happen?" Believers ask the question slightly differently: "Why did God *allow* this to happen?" Christians phrase the question this way because they do not allow for meaningless events, because at the heart of the Christian worldview is the assurance that everything in history has a purpose in the mind of almighty God. God is not chaotic or random. For everything there is a purpose—including those events we define as tragedies.

In the days after September 11, there were comments from some well-known preachers, particularly Jerry Falwell, regarding possible reasons God allowed the attacks. He made the observation that this tragedy was God's act of judgment on America for its immorality, for its tolerance of abortion, for its destruction of the human family, and for its stances on other moral issues of our day. That statement created a firestorm of controversy, and even Christian commentators were quite vocal in their criticism of this assessment. In the end, Falwell publicly recanted his statement. It is always unwise to jump to conclusions about the "why" of our suffering.

Now, if someone were to say to me, "Why did God allow this to happen?" the only honest answer I could give would be "I don't know." I can't read God's mind. I don't know that it was an act of judgment. On the other hand, I can't think of anything in the Christian worldview that would rule out the possibility that it was an act of judgment. It is clear in Scripture that God has brought calamities on nations as an act of judgment from time to time, but it is impossible to know whether the events of September 11 were, in fact, His judgment for He has not told us. Now, if you were to ask me whether God was involved, I would say yes, because I'm committed to the Christian doctrine of providence. I'm convinced that God was involved in this event and that it happened according to His purpose. But what the specific purpose was, I have no idea.

The bottom-line assumption for anyone who believes in the God of providence is that ultimately there are no tragedies. God has promised that all things that happen—all pain, all suffering, all tragedies—are but for a moment, and that He works in and through these events for the good of those who love Him (Rom. 8:28). That's why the apostle Paul said that the pain, the suffering, the affliction that we bear in this world isn't worthy to be compared, isn't worthy to be mentioned in the same breath, with the glory and the blessedness that God has stored up for His people (Rom. 8:18).

THE BENEFITS OF CONSIDERING GOD'S WORK

Sometimes it seems that earlier generations of Christians had a higher view of God than we do. The reason for that may very well lie in the fact that they were much more familiar with pain, with suffering, with persecution, and with death than we are. Because of all they endured, they were forced to consider the hand of God in the midst of their difficulties.

The bottom line is that God's hand is in affliction. His sovereignty is manifest in the dark side of life. This is said so frequently in Scripture that it is amazing that it is so hard for us to get it. I believe that the reason for this is that we shut our minds from thinking about these things. Why do we go to the house of mirth in the first place? For many of us, a party is not simply an opportunity to have a good time but a chance to get away from thinking, to get away from considering our "life situation." We look for an escape, an avenue of pleasure that will somehow dull the fears and the aches that we carry about. But the wise person looks for the finger of God in the house of mirth as well as in the house of mourning, in all things that take place.

It is interesting to consider how Solomon begins chapter 8 of Ecclesiastes. Having just affirmed these difficult truths regarding God's sovereignty, he writes: "Who is like a wise man? And who knows the interpretation of a thing? A man's wisdom makes his face shine, and the sternness of his face is changed" (v. 1). After hearing Solomon tell us it is better to go to the house of mourning than to the house of mirth, we might get the idea that God wants His people to be so contemplative, so considering in the difficult things of life, that they walk around stone-faced, with a dour disposition. That is not at all what the author of Ecclesiastes intends. Instead, he is affirming here that when we understand the sovereignty of God, it changes the countenance of our face. It changes our demeanor. Those who understand God's sovereignty have joy even in the midst of suffering, a joy reflected on their very faces, for they see that their suffering is not without purpose.

CHAPTER FIVE

THE FINAL
CALLING

M y eyes were riveted to the clock on the waiting room wall. It was a
sterile timepiece with no ornamentation. Designed for pure utility, its
sole purpose was to display the current moment in world history.

Behind closed doors, people were suspended in time. For some, the minutes that were passing were the final minutes of life.

I was among those waiting. Families were gathered in to hold vigil for
loved ones. They waited for news of the outcomes of various surgeries.

I stared at the clock again. The clock was telling a story. I did not like its
message. The operation was taking too long. The surgery was supposed to be
corrective and "routine." There was no cause for alarm. This type of surgery
was done countless times with no adverse results. But it was taking too long.

More time passed. Then, at last, the surgeon appeared. He was still
dressed in his green uniform. "Mr. Sproul?" he said. "We ran into some com-
plications. I'm afraid that we have discovered a tumor that we didn't expect.
The final results will have to come from pathology, but there is little doubt
that it is malignant."

His words were like a kick in the stomach, but I calmly asked the question I wanted to scream: "What's the prognosis?"

"I'm afraid that it's not good. We can try chemotherapy, but to be frank, all we can really hope for is some time. This form of cancer is virulent. It is almost always fatal."

"How much time, Doctor?" I asked.

"We can never say for sure. Six months to a year. Perhaps more if the therapy is effective."

"Does she know?" I asked.

"No, not yet. She's in the recovery room and is heavily sedated. I plan to tell her tomorrow. I would appreciate it if you could be with her when I give my report. I will be in about one."

I had difficulty sleeping that night. I was frightened. My studies in theology gave me no practical knowledge about how to deal with such a disease. How do you announce to someone that he or she has a terminal illness? Do you disguise the truth? Do you hold out false hope? Do you suggest the possibility of a miracle that God may not be pleased to grant?

I approached my friend's room the next afternoon with apprehension. When I entered, she was remarkably alert and outwardly serene. Her eyes told me, however, that somehow she already knew.

The doctor was kind and gentle, yet forthright. "I don't like what we found yesterday," he said. In a gracious manner, he explained exactly what it was. He set forth the procedures for chemotherapy. He explained the damage that already had been done to vital organs.

I sensed that among the three of us in the room, the patient had the calmest spirit. She spoke to comfort us. "It's all right," she said. "I'm ready for what God has in store for me."

My friend lived for two years, surprising everyone, including the doctors. She remained productive. She visited Israel. She got her house in order. She cared for her family. She died with grace and dignity.

During those two years, we had many conversations. We prayed together. We cried together. We laughed together. She gave me elaborate instructions for her funeral. She discussed her will with me.

This woman was a Christian. She viewed her final months in this world as a vocation. She prepared herself mentally and spiritually for death. She viewed death as not just the *end* of life, but as a *part* of life. It was an experience she had never had before. It was the final experience of life that every person must undergo.

DEATH AS A VOCATION

We have considered suffering as a vocation. Dare we think of death as a vocation, too?

The author of Ecclesiastes made this declaration: "To everything there is a season, a time for every purpose under heaven: a time to be born, and a time to die" (Eccl. 3:1–2a). Likewise the author of Hebrews says, "It is appointed for men to die once, but after this the judgment" (Heb. 9:27).

Notice the language of Scripture. It speaks of death in terms of a "purpose under heaven" and of an "appointment." Death is a divine appointment. It is part of God's purpose for our lives. God calls each person to die. He is sovereign over all of life, including the final experience of life.

We usually limit the idea of vocation to our careers or our jobs. The word *vocation*, however, comes from the Latin word *vocare*, meaning "to call." Used in the Christian sense, vocation refers to a divine calling, a summons that comes from God Himself. He calls people to teach, to preach, to sing, to make cars, and to change diapers. There are as many vocations as there are facets to human life.

We have different vocations with respect to the jobs and tasks God gives us in this life. But we all share in the vocation of death. Every one of us is called to die. That vocation is as much a calling from God as is a "call" to the ministry of Christ. Sometimes the call comes suddenly and without warning. Sometimes it comes with advance notification. But it comes to all of us. And it comes from God.

I am aware that there are teachers who tell us that God has nothing to do with death. Death is seen strictly as the fiendish device of the Devil. All pain, suffering, disease, and tragedy are blamed on the Evil One. God is absolved of any responsibility. This view is designed to make sure that God is free of blame for anything that goes wrong in this world. "God always wills healing," we are told. If that healing does not happen, then the fault lies with Satan—or with us. Death, they say, is not in the plan of God. It represents a victory for Satan over the realm of God.

Such views may bring temporary relief to the afflicted. But they are not true. They have nothing to do with biblical Christianity. They are intended to absolve God of any blame, but they contradict His sovereignty.

Yes, there is a Devil. He is our archenemy. He will do anything in his power to bring misery into our lives. But Satan is not sovereign. Satan does not hold the keys of death.

When Jesus appeared in a vision to the apostle John on the Isle of Patmos, He identified Himself with these words: "Do not be afraid; I am the First and the Last. I am He who lives, and was dead, and behold, I am alive forevermore. Amen. And I have the keys of Hades and of Death" (Rev. 1:17–18).

Jesus holds the keys to death, and Satan cannot snatch those keys out of His hand. Christ's grip is firm. He holds the keys because He owns the keys. All authority in heaven and on earth has been given to Him. That includes all authority over life and death. The angel of death is at His beck and call.

World history has witnessed the emergence of many forms of religious dualism. Dualism affirms the existence of two equal and opposite forces. These forces are variously called good and evil, God and Satan, Yin and Yang. The two forces are locked in eternal combat. Since they are equal as well as opposite, the conflict goes on forever, with neither side ever gaining the upper hand. The world is doomed to serve as the eternal battleground between these hostile forces. We are the victims of their struggle, the pawns in their eternal chess game.

Dualism is on a collision course with Christianity. The Christian faith has no stock in dualism. Satan may be *opposed* to God, but he is by no means *equal* to God. Satan is a creature; God is the Creator. Satan is potent; God is omnipotent. Satan is knowledgeable and crafty; God is omniscient. Satan is localized in his presence; God is omnipresent. Satan is finite; God is infinite.

The list could go on. But it is clear from Scripture that Satan is not an ultimate force in any sense.

We are not doomed to an ultimate conflict with no hope of resolution. The message of Scripture is one of victory—full, final, and ultimate victory. It is not our doom that is certain, but Satan's. His head has been crushed by the heel of Christ, who is the Alpha and Omega.

Above all suffering and death stands the crucified and risen Lord. He has defeated the ultimate enemy of life. He has vanquished the power of death. He calls us to die, a call to obedience in the final transition of life. Because of Christ, death is not final. It is a passage from one world to the next.

God does not always will healing. If He did, He would suffer endless frustration, seeing His will being repeatedly thwarted in the deaths of His people. He did not will the healing of Stephen from the wounds inflicted by the stones that were hurled against him. He did not will the healing of Moses, of Joseph, of David, of Paul, of Augustine, of Martin Luther, of John Calvin. These all died in faith. Ultimate healing comes through death and after death.

Teachers argue that there is healing in the atonement of Christ. Indeed there is. Jesus bore all of our sins on the cross. Yet none of us is free from sin in this life. Likewise, none of us is free from sickness in this life. The healing that is in the cross is real. We participate in its benefits now, in this life. But the fullness of the healing from both sin and disease takes place in heaven. We still must die at our appointed times.

Certainly God answers prayers and gives healings to our bodies during this life. But even these healings are temporary. Jesus raised Lazarus from the dead. But Lazarus died again. Jesus gave sight to the blind and hearing to the deaf. Yet every person Jesus healed eventually died. They died not because Satan finally won over Jesus, but because Jesus called them to die.

When God issues a call to us, it is always a holy call. The vocation of dying is a sacred vocation. To understand that is one of the most important lessons a Christian can ever learn. When the summons comes, we can respond in many ways. We can become angry, bitter, or terrified. But if we see it as a call from God and not a threat from Satan, we are far more prepared to cope with its difficulties.

FINISHING THE RACE

I will never forget the last words my father spoke to me. We were seated together on the living room sofa. His body had been ravaged by three strokes. One side of his face was distorted by paralysis. His left eye and left lip drooped uncontrollably. He spoke to me with a heavy slur. His words were difficult to understand, but their meaning was crystal clear. He uttered these words: "I have fought the good fight, I have finished the race, I have kept the faith" (2 Tim. 4:7).

These were the last words he ever spoke to me. Hours later, he suffered his fourth and final cerebral hemorrhage. I found him collapsed on the floor, a trickle of blood oozing from the corner of his mouth. He was comatose. Mercifully, he died a day and a half later without regaining consciousness.

His last words to me were heroic. My last words to him were cowardly. I protested his words of premonition. I said rudely, "Don't say that, Dad!"

I have said many things in my life that I desperately wish I had not said, but none of my words are more shameful to me now than those. But words can no more be recalled than a speeding arrow after the bow string has snapped in full release.

My words were a rebuke to my father. I refused to allow him the dignity of a final testimony to me. He knew he was dying. I refused to accept what he had already accepted with grace.

I was seventeen. I knew nothing of the business of dying. It was not a very good year. I watched my father die an inch at a time over a period of three years. I never heard him complain. I never heard him protest. He sat in the same chair day after day, week after week, year after year. He read the Bible with a large magnifying glass. I was blind to the anxieties that must have plagued him. He could not work, so there was no income, and we had no disability insurance. He sat there, waiting to die, watching his life savings trickle away with his own life.

I was angry at God. My father was angry at no one. He lived out his last days faithful to his vocation. He fought the good fight. A good fight is a fight fought without hostility, without bitterness, without self-pity. I had never been in a fight like that.

My father finished the race. I was not even in the starting blocks. He ran the race God had called him to run. He ran until his legs crumbled. But somehow he kept going. When he couldn't walk anymore, he still was at the table each night for dinner. He asked me to help him. It was a daily ritual. Each evening, I went to his room, where he was seated in that same chair. I stooped backward, facing away from him so that he could drape his arms around my neck and shoulders. I clasped his wrists together and stood, lifting him up from the chair. Then I dragged him to the dining room table. He finished the race. My only consolation is that I was able to help him. I was with him at the finish line.

I carried him one last time. When I found him unconscious on the floor, somehow I managed to get him into the bed where he died. On that trip, he could not help me drag him. He could not put his arms around my neck. It took effort mixed with adrenalin to get him from the floor to the bed. But I had to get him there. It was unthinkable to me that he should die on the floor.

When my father died, I was not a Christian. Faith was something beyond my experience and my understanding. When my father said, "I have kept the faith," I missed the weight of his words. I shut them out. I had no idea that he was quoting the apostle Paul's final message to his beloved disciple, Timothy. My father's eloquent testimony was wasted on me at the time. But not now; now I understand. Now I want to persevere as my father persevered. I want to run the race and finish the course as he did before me. I have no desire to suffer as he suffered, but I want to keep the faith as he kept it.

If my father taught me anything, he taught me how to die. The events I have just described left an indelible mark on me. For years after my father died, I had a recurring nightmare. The dream had a vivid intensity. I would see my father alive again. Thus, the beginning of the dream was thrilling. In my slumber, the impossible became real. He was alive! But my joy would change quickly to despair as I grasped the fullness of his appearance in my dream. He was crippled and paralyzed. He was hopelessly and helplessly dying. The scene was never that of a healthy, vibrant father, but of a father caught in the throes of death.

Whenever I had this nightmare, I would wake up sweating with a sick, empty feeling in the pit of my stomach. Only as I studied the Scriptures did I discover that death is not like that. Only when I discovered the content of the Christian faith did the nightmares finally cease.

PASSING THROUGH THE VALLEY OF THE SHADOW

When God gives us a vocation to die, He sends us on a mission. The course may be frightening. It is an obstacle course with pitfalls along the way. We wonder if we will have the courage to make our way to the finish line, for the trail takes us through the valley of the shadow.

The valley of the shadow of death is a valley where the sun's rays often seem to be blotted out. To approach it is to tremble. We would prefer to walk around it, to seek a safe bypass. But men and women of faith can enter that valley without fear. David told us how: "Yea, though I walk through the valley of the shadow of death, I will fear no evil; for You are with me; Your rod and Your staff, they comfort me" (Ps. 23:4).

David was a shepherd. In this psalm, David put himself in the place of the sheep. He saw himself as a lamb under the care of the Great Shepherd. He entered the valley without fear for one overarching reason—the Shepherd went with him. He trusted himself to the care and the protection of the Shepherd.

The lamb found comfort in the Shepherd's weapons, the rod and the staff. The ancient shepherd was armed. He could use the crook of his staff to rescue a fallen lamb from a pit. He could wield his rod against hostile beasts that sought to devour his sheep. Without the shepherd, the sheep would have been helpless in the shadowy valley. But as long as the shepherd was present, the sheep had nothing to fear.

If a bear or lion attacked and killed the shepherd, the sheep would scatter.

They would be vulnerable to the lion's jaws. If the shepherd fell, all was lost for the sheep.

But we have a Shepherd who *cannot* fall and who *will not* abandon his flock at the first sign of trouble. Our Shepherd is armed with omnipotent force. He is not threatened by the valley of shadows. He is Lord of the valley.

David's confidence was rooted in the absolute certainty of the presence of God. He understood that with a divine vocation comes divine assistance and the absolute promise of the divine presence. God will not send us where He refuses to go Himself.

My best friend in college and seminary was a man named Don McClure. Don was the son of pioneer missionaries. He had grown up in the remote interior of Africa. Don personally had discovered several tribes of primitive natives; he was the first white man they had ever seen. He had killed spitting cobras in his bedroom. He had had a close encounter with a crocodile that had literally jumped into his small canoe with him. He had been rescued by his father at the last minute when he was surrounded by a hungry pack of lions.

I keep a newspaper clipping in my Bible that reports the martyrdom of Don's father. Don and his father were camped in a remote area of Ethiopia. During the night, they were awakened by a surprise attack from communist guerrillas. Don and his father were captured and dragged before a firing squad. Don stood next to his father when the guerrillas opened fire. First they shot Don's dad, killing him instantly. Don heard the shot and saw the flame from the rifle that was pointed at him from six feet away. He fell next to his father, shocked to realize that he was still alive.

In the confusion of the night, the guerrillas fled as quickly as they had appeared. Don hugged the ground, feigning death until all was quiet. He had suffered only minor flesh wounds, though he was covered with powder burns. Fighting the impulse to flee, Don remained long enough to dig a shallow grave with his bare hands. There he committed his father's body to the ground.

I called Don "Tarzan" because his life mirrored the legends of Johnny Weissmuller. He was (to this day) the most fearless person I ever met. If I were trapped in a foxhole behind enemy lines in combat, I would want Don McClure with me. I would be proud to have him at my side in the valley of the shadow. But I have One who is greater than Don who promises to go through that valley with me.

God is our refuge and our strength in times of trouble. His promise is not only that He will go with us into the valley. Even more important is His promise of what lies on the other side of the valley. God promises to go with us for the entire journey in order to guide us to what lies beyond. The valley of the shadow of death is not a box canyon. It is a passageway to a better country. The valley leads to life—life far more abundant than anything we can imagine. The goal of the vocation of death is heaven itself. But there is no route to heaven except through this valley.

David also understood that. Though he lived before Christ, before the resurrection, before the New Testament revelation of glory, nevertheless God had not been altogether silent on the matter. Already there was the hope of the "bosom of Abraham" (Luke 16:22).

David confessed his faith in this manner: "I would have lost heart, unless I had believed that I would see the goodness of the LORD in the land of the living" (Ps. 27:13).

The God of Abraham, Isaac, and Jacob is the God of the living. The God of David is the God of the living. The God of Jesus is the God of the living. There is life beyond the shadow of death.

Both my friend and my father ran a race because God called them to run the race. They finished the course because God was with them through every obstacle. They kept the faith because He kept them.

This was a powerful legacy. It is the legacy the risen Christ gives to all of His sheep.

CHAPTER SIX

DYING IN FAITH

The question that plagues us about death is not *if* we will die. There is a macabre joke that holds that there are only two certain things in life—death and taxes. But some people manage to avoid or evade taxes. The only way we can possibly avoid death is to remain alive until the return of Christ.

I just had to change the words of the previous sentence. At first I wrote these words: "The only way we can possibly avoid death is to *be alive at* the return of Christ." I changed the wording because my original sentence was at least misleading and at worst heretical. The New Testament assures us that all who are in Christ will certainly be alive at His coming. If we die before He returns, we will be raised to witness His glorious return:

> But I do not want you to be ignorant, brethren, concerning those who have fallen asleep, lest you sorrow as others who have no hope. For if we believe that Jesus died and rose again, even so God will bring with Him those who sleep in Jesus.
>
> For this we say to you by the word of the Lord, that we who are alive and remain until the coming of the Lord will by no means precede those

who are asleep. For the Lord Himself will descend from heaven with a shout, with the voice of an archangel, and with the trumpet of God. And the dead in Christ will rise first.

Then we who are alive and remain shall be caught up together with them in the clouds to meet the Lord in the air. And thus we shall always be with the Lord.

Therefore comfort one another with these words. (1 Thess. 4:13–18)

Here the apostle Paul gives a vivid description of what is popularly called the rapture of the saints. No Christian will miss the rapture. Those who remain alive until it happens will have no advantage over those who have already died. The dead in Christ will be raised for this event.

I remember as a child having to go to bed before the Fourth of July fireworks display. I didn't want to go to sleep for fear that I would miss all the fun. My parents overcame my anxiety by promising me that they would wake me in time to see the fireworks. They kept their promise.

None of us saw the birth of Christ. We missed His dazzling display of miracles during His earthly ministry. Likewise, nobody alive today beheld Christ's agony on the cross. None of us was an eyewitness of His glorious resurrection and ascension into heaven. But no Christian will sleep through the second coming of Christ. Though we did not see His first coming, we all will be eyewitnesses of His return. The climax of the exaltation of Jesus will be viewed by every believer. God will raise the dead to make certain that every eye shall behold His triumphant return.

This event circumscribes the only "if" about our dying.

THE GREAT DIVIDE: DYING IN FAITH OR IN SIN

We have many questions about our own deaths. We wonder *where* we will die. We ponder *when* we will die. We ask *why* we will die. The chief concern of Scripture, however, is *how* we will die. This is the big question, the question that is loaded with significance.

I once received a note from my theological mentor, Dr. John Gerstner. In that note, he passed on to me the news that a mutual friend had succumbed to cancer. Gerstner's simple but poignant words were these: "Tom Graham died in faith." Those five words said a lot to me. Gerstner was saying that Tom died as a Christian. Tom remained faithful to the end.

Scripture has much to say about *how* we die. No, the Bible does not deal with specific causes of death. We know that we can die of cancer, from a heart attack, from strangulation, from a gunshot wound, or from a host of other mortal causes. But these possible causes of biological death are not the chief concern of Scripture.

When Scripture speaks of the *how* of death, the focus is on the spiritual state of the person at the time of his death. Here we see the "how" of death reduced to only two options. We either die in faith or we die in our sins:

"Son of man, I have made you a watchman for the house of Israel; therefore hear a word from My mouth, and give them warning from Me: When I say to the wicked, 'You shall surely die,' and you give him no warning, nor speak to warn the wicked from his wicked way, to save his life, that same wicked man shall die in his iniquity; but his blood I will require at your hand. Yet, if you warn the wicked, and he does not turn from his wickedness, nor from his wicked way, he shall die in his iniquity; but you have delivered your soul." (Ezek. 3:17–19)

What Ezekiel declared in the Old Testament, Jesus reaffirmed in the New Testament: "Therefore I said to you that you will die in your sins; for if you do not believe that I am He, you will die in your sins" (John 8:24).

We sometimes think that the worst thing that can befall a person is to die. That is not the message of Jesus. According to Christ, the worst possible thing that can befall us is to die in our sins.

This is the biblical message that is so widely ignored in our day. We like to believe that everyone who dies automatically goes to heaven. We assume that the only ticket required for entrance into the kingdom of God is death. The warning required by Ezekiel is ignored because we do not believe it is necessary.

THE NEED FOR WORDS OF WARNING

I once had the opportunity of speaking with Billy Graham. During our conversation, I mentioned to him an experience I had as a college student. I recalled standing around a television set in the men's dormitory in the late 1950s. Some of us had gathered to watch a television show on which Dr. Graham was being interviewed.

When the host interviewed Dr. Graham, he tried to keep the interview light and humorous. He joked about the state of his own soul. Dr. Graham kept his poise and, with dignity and grace, told the host on national television that he needed Christ.

Thirty years later, I asked Dr. Graham about that episode. He replied that he had kept in touch with the host and reminded him of his need for Christ. Dr. Graham really cared about that man and did not want him to die in his sins.

Speaking to a dying person about his need for a Savior is not an easy matter. The last thing we want to do to a person in such a condition is to disturb him in any way or to make him feel uncomfortable. We naturally think that it is an act of human kindness not to discuss such matters.

But God commands us to speak to the dying about their need for a Savior. Ezekiel makes that crystal clear. If we love people, we will warn them of the consequences of dying in their sins.

We remember the complaints that Jeremiah brought before God. Jeremiah was upset because God had called him to give the people a warning they did not want to hear. To make matters worse for Jeremiah, his ministry was being undermined by false prophets who were very popular because they told the people what they wanted to hear. They declared, "Peace, peace" when there was no peace (Jer. 8:11).

Speaking for God, Jeremiah declared: "Do not listen to the words of the prophets who prophesy to you. They make you worthless; they speak a vision of their own heart, not from the mouth of the LORD. They continually say to those who despise Me, 'The LORD has said, "You shall have peace"'; and to everyone who walks according to the dictates of his own heart, they say, 'No evil shall come upon you'" (Jer. 23:16–17).

The message of the false prophets served only to heal the hurts of the people *slightly* (Jer. 8:11). False words of comfort are like putting a Band-Aid on a gaping wound. The healing is at best slight. The false prophets were giving a crude form of slight relief instead of the authentic balm of Gilead.

The great lie is the one that declares there is no last judgment. Yet if Jesus of Nazareth taught anything, He emphatically taught that there would be a last judgment. We do not respect Jesus as a teacher if we ignore His instruction on this matter. Consider these words of Christ:

> "When the Son of Man comes in His glory, and all the holy angels with Him, then He will sit on the throne of His glory. All the nations will be gathered before Him, and He will separate them one from another, as a shepherd divides his sheep from the goats. And He will set the sheep on His right hand, but the goats on the left. Then the King will say to those on His right hand, 'Come, you blessed of My Father, inherit the Kingdom prepared for you from the foundation of the world.' . . . Then He will also say to those on the left hand, 'Depart from Me, you cursed, into the everlasting fire prepared for the devil and his angels.' . . . And these will go away into everlasting punishment, but the righteous into eternal life." (Matt. 25:31–46)

Here Jesus uttered sober words of warning. Those who die in their sins will be separated; they will be numbered with the goats.

Jesus amplified this warning elsewhere. He warned that "nothing is secret that will not be revealed, nor anything hidden that will not be known and come to light" (Luke 8:17). He also said: "There is nothing covered that will not be revealed, nor hidden that will not be known. Therefore whatever you have spoken in the dark will be heard in the light, and what you have spoken in the ear in inner rooms will be proclaimed on the housetops" (Luke 12:2–3).

Jesus warned that a day will come when all secrets will become known. It will be the final end to all the cover-ups of this world. Every closet will be opened and the skeletons will be made plainly visible. The sins of us all will be made known unless we are "covered" by the cloak of Christ's righteousness.

This future day of nakedness is a day when those who die in their sins will "say to the mountains, 'Fall on us!' and to the hills, 'Cover us!'" (Luke 23:30).

FLEEING THE WRATH TO COME

The New Testament describes Jesus as "Savior." The name *Jesus* was announced by the archangel Gabriel when he visited Mary. An angelic message to Joseph confirmed this name: "And she will bring forth a Son, and you shall call His name JESUS, for He will save His people from their sins" (Matt. 1:21).

The salvation of which the Bible speaks has a specific goal. The term *salvation* in general can be used for many things. Any type of rescue from danger or calamity can be called salvation. Biblically, a person can be saved from a disease or from financial disaster. If any army escapes defeat in battle, it experiences salvation.

But the salvation wrought by Jesus is not of this general type. It is specific. Jesus saves us "from the wrath to come" (1 Thess. 1:10).

The preaching of John the Baptist accented this warning about the future. John spoke harshly to the Pharisees and Sadducees, the clergy of his day, saying, "Who warned you to flee from the wrath to come?" (Matt. 3:7). The warning that was given to first-century Israel is the same warning that is so woefully neglected in our own day.

I once overheard a conversation between two men. They were discussing the sermon preached by a guest minister in a Presbyterian church. The first asked, "How was the preacher on Sunday?"

The second man replied: "He was an old-fashioned preacher. He preached about fire and brimstone."

What qualified the preacher as "old-fashioned" was that he preached on the last judgment. The concept of the judgment was deemed to be out of date. This is not an uncommon viewpoint. It is not fashionable to speak in our culture about a final judgment.

I am sure that similar conversations were happening in Jesus' day. Some who listened to the preaching of John the Baptist and of Jesus surely called them "old-fashioned." Perhaps the people said something like this: "Oh, these guys are old-fashioned. They speak like the Old Testament prophets."

It is strange that we are so quick to dismiss as "old-fashioned" any mention of a final judgment. It is especially strange that it happens in a time and a culture that is so concerned about justice. We have worked for civil justice, for social justice, and for international justice. Yet we observe what the philosopher Immanuel Kant so acutely observed: justice does not always prevail in this world.

The God of the Bible is a God of justice. His own character is just. Therefore, for God not to correct injustices in this world, to let the scales of justice remain forever out of balance, would be for Him to compromise His own integrity. This is precisely what He refuses to do. He promises ultimate justice.

FINAL JUSTICE AND FINAL JUDGMENT

The Judge of all the earth cannot bring forth final justice without a final judgment. He insists that all human beings will be held accountable for their actions. If we are not ultimately accountable, then the only conclusion we can reach is that ultimately we don't count. The bottom line would be that it doesn't matter ultimately how we live our lives. But every one of us knows that it *does* matter how people live. It matters to me how people treat me. It matters to you how people treat you.

Each one of us has been a victim of injustice at one point or another. Likewise, each one of us has committed injustices to other people. The reason we experience and commit such injustice is because, as sinners, we are unjust people.

The dilemma we face is this: God is just. We are unjust. This is the worst dilemma a human being can face. For a guilty person to face the justice meted out in our criminal justice system is one thing. To stand before the tribunal of God is something else. We cry out with David, "If You, LORD, should mark iniquities, who could stand?" (Ps. 130:3). David's question is rhetorical in nature. The answer is obvious: *no one* will be able to stand.

The central issue of Christianity is the issue of justification. It faces the dilemma squarely. The only possible way for an unjust person to stand in the presence of a just and holy God is to be justified. If we remain unjustified, we die in our sins.

The only way we can be justified is by the righteousness of Christ. He alone has the merit necessary to cover us. That righteousness is received by faith. If we trust in Christ, we are covered by His righteousness and are justified by faith. If we do not trust in Christ, we will stand before God's judgment alone, unjust people before a just God.

You may be thinking: "I am not an unjust person. I have never murdered anybody. I have never stolen anything that was not mine." Indeed, if you are perfectly just, you have no need of a Savior. If you've never broken the law of God, you have nothing to fear from His judgment.

However, we suffer from two grand delusions. The first delusion is that we are good enough to stand in the presence of a perfectly righteous God. It is a delusion because every one of us has sinned. We have to be perfectly free of sin and perfectly righteous in order to stand before God. We are deluding ourselves in the extreme if we think we are perfect.

Only a few people become deluded enough to think that they are without sin. This is not the delusion most of us suffer. It is the second delusion that catches so many of us. The fact that God is just and that we are unjust doesn't seem to bother us. We nurture the hope that since God is loving and merciful, He will make room for us in heaven even if we never repent of our sins and embrace Christ as Savior. We think that faith is not a necessary condition for salvation.

This delusion hurls an insult at the mercy of God. It assumes that by crucifying His only begotten Son for us, God did not do enough. It concludes that His requirements of faith and trust in the atoning Savior are a bit narrow.

The author of Hebrews labored to warn his readers of the consequences that flow from ignoring the priestly act of atonement rendered by Jesus. He raised another rhetorical question: "How shall we escape if we neglect so great a salvation, which at the first began to be spoken by the Lord, and was confirmed to us by those who heard Him?" (Heb. 2:3).

This warning is followed by further admonitions: "Beware, brethren, lest there be in any of you an evil heart of unbelief in departing from the living God; but exhort one another daily, while it is called 'Today,' lest any of you be hardened through the deceitfulness of sin. . . . And to whom did He swear that they would not enter His rest, but to those who did not obey? So we see that they could not enter in because of unbelief" (Heb. 3:12–19).

I don't know when it is that you are reading this book. I have no way of knowing what the date is on the calendar. But whatever day of the week or month it is, one thing is certain: you are reading these words today. We notice that the admonition of Hebrews is for *today*. If our neglect continues until tomorrow, it may be too late.

The warning of Scripture stresses that as long as we delay repentance and faith, we run the risk of being "hardened" through the deceitfulness of sin. We've heard the gospel preached so often that we can become calloused to it. Our hearts can become calcified; our consciences can be seared. That is how sin works. First we excuse ourselves and seek all manner of self-justification. Finally we deceive ourselves into thinking that faith and repentance are not necessary.

THE NECESSITY OF NOT DELAYING

God says that repentance and faith are necessary, utterly necessary. Hebrews declares that God is so serious about this that He swore a vow not to let the disobedient enter into His rest. Never was a more sacred oath sworn. It is the worst kind of delusion to even entertain the possibility that God might not keep this vow.

The author of Hebrews concluded by saying, "So we see that they could not enter in because of unbelief" (Heb. 3:19). If a person remains in unbelief, it is simply not possible for him to enter into the rest of God. Unbelief is a barrier to heaven.

We see, then, that there are only two ways of dying. We can die in faith or we can die in our sins.

Many people hold out hope for a second chance after death. The Roman Catholic Church nurtures this hope with the doctrine of purgatory. Purgatory is a place of "purging" for those who need some cleansing before entering heaven. Therefore, Masses are said and prayers are offered for the dead. (It is official Roman Catholic teaching that those in purgatory are baptized Christians who eventually will enter heaven. However, it seems that in the popular imagination of many Catholics and others, purgatory is where sinners are given a second chance to mend their ways and make it to heaven.)

If ever a doctrine was invented to meet the needs of a frightened humanity, it is the doctrine of purgatory. But Scripture offers not a shred of evidence to support the idea. On the contrary, the urgent focus of Scripture is on the necessity of repentance *before* we die. Again the author of Hebrews declares, "It is appointed for men to die once, but after this the judgment" (Heb. 9:27).

I remember with much affection my uncle who lived in our home when I was growing up. He was a tough man with bulging muscles and a profane mouth. I vividly recall that he always seemed to have a solid black layer of grease visible under his fingernails. My uncle had no time for religion or church. He thought that religion was for sissies.

When I announced that I was going to seminary to prepare for the ministry, my uncle almost had an apoplexy. He teased me relentlessly. He joked that soon I'd be wearing my collar backward and would walk around in a black shirt.

Shortly after my ordination, my uncle became terminally ill. About a week before he died, I visited him in his room. He was dying and he knew it. Now there were no jokes. He was seriously concerned about where he was going. He said to me, "I'm not ready to go."

We talked about Christ. My uncle made a serious profession of faith. He got matters settled between himself and God. He died in faith.

Just as God swore an oath that the impenitent will not enter His rest, so He swore that those who repent and believe in Christ *will* enter His rest. Again the author of Hebrews elaborated: "Therefore, since a promise remains of entering His rest, let us fear lest any of you seem to have come short of it. . . . For we who have believed do enter that rest" (Heb. 4:1–3a).

Hebrews 4 concludes with these words:

> Seeing then that we have a great High Priest who has passed through the heavens, Jesus the Son of God, let us hold fast our confession. For we do not have a High Priest who cannot sympathize with our weaknesses, but was in all points tempted as we are, yet without sin. Let us therefore come boldly to the throne of grace, that we may obtain mercy and find grace to help in time of need. (Heb. 4:14–16)

If we die in faith, we join a great assembly of those who have gone before us. Hebrews provides a litany of the heroes of faith:

> By faith Abel offered to God a more excellent sacrifice. . . . By faith Enoch was taken away. . . . By faith Noah, being divinely warned of things not yet seen, moved with godly fear, prepared an ark. . . . By faith Abraham obeyed when he was called to go out to the place which he would receive as an inheritance. And he went out, not knowing where he was going. . . . By faith Sarah herself also received strength to conceive seed. . . . These all died in faith, not having received the promises, but having seen them afar off were assured of them, embraced them and confessed that they were strangers and pilgrims on the earth. For those who say such things declare plainly that they seek a homeland. And truly if they had called to mind that country from which they had come out, they would have had opportunity to return. But now they desire a better, that is, a heavenly country. Therefore God is not ashamed to be called their God, for He has prepared a city for them. (Heb. 11:4–11, 13–16)

If we die in faith, we will join Abel, Noah, Abraham and many others who lived and died in faith. We will be counted among those of whom God is not ashamed to be called their God. The city He has prepared for them will be ours, too.

The rest of this book will focus on two major concerns. The first is: *Is there really a heaven?* The second is: *What is heaven like?*

PART TWO

After Death

CHAPTER SEVEN

SPECULATIONS
ON LIFE AFTER DEATH

S ome years ago, I visited with my aunt, who had been born in 1900. It
was a time of reminiscence, of nostalgia. I asked her all sorts of questions
about our roots and family history. She leaned back in her rocking chair and
spoke with misty eyes of the old days. As she spoke, she filled in some gaps in
my knowledge about my father's life and my grandparents' lives.

The highlight of this excursion through history was my aunt's recollec-
tions of my great-grandfather, Charles Sproul (the origin of the "C" in my
own name, Robert Charles). He was born in County Donegal, Ireland, in
1824. He arrived in this country in 1843 with no shoes on his feet, having
left a thatched-roof cottage with a mud floor in the old country. During the
Civil War, he was Fireman Third Class Sproul aboard the U.S.S. *Grampus* in
the Union Navy. He fought at the Battle of Vicksburg. He died in 1910 at
the age of eighty-six.

This conversation with my aunt took place in the summer of 1987, 163
years after my great-grandfather was born. When Charles Sproul died, he had

been living at the home of my grandfather in Pittsburgh. My aunt knew him for ten years before he died.

It was a spooky feeling to talk to someone who had vivid memories of a person who was born in 1824. So much time, so much history, has transpired since that date. I wondered what it would be like if I lived to be eighty-six and could tell my great-grandchildren the stories I heard, first person, from someone who knew my great-grandfather. I will be eighty-six in the year 2025, so such a conversation would span a time frame of more than two centuries.

When Charles Sproul was born, the United States was only a few decades old. James Monroe was President. Abraham Lincoln was still a teenager. There was no transcontinental railroad, no automobiles, no airplanes, no radios, no televisions, not even an electric light bulb. The world has changed.

Charles Sproul is gone. His son, Robert, married a girl who had traveled up the Ohio River from Ohio to Pittsburgh by steamboat. Robert died in 1945. His sons, including my father, both died in 1956.

My son was born in 1965. His name, like mine, is Robert. He has two sons who are carrying on the family name. If they have sons, the family name will endure for at least another generation. If not, the family name will die.

The Bible says that "all flesh is grass" (Isa. 40:6). It grows, but then it withers and dies.

A man once asked me about my "long-term goals." He said, "What do you want to be doing with your life in five years? In ten years?" The question gave me pause. To a teenager, five years seems like eternity, but it hardly seems like a long time frame to me.

A more relevant question for me is, "What will I be doing one hundred years from now?" It may seem like a silly question. It sounds almost like the question, "What was I doing one hundred years ago?" One hundred years ago I didn't exist. My sister didn't exist. My father didn't exist. Old Charles Sproul did exist, and so did his son, Robert. But they are gone, as I will be gone one hundred years from now.

Few if any people reading this book were alive one hundred years ago. Almost certainly no one who reads this book will be alive one hundred years from now.

Or will they? Do we have a future that will last one hundred years and beyond?

THE QUEST FOR KNOWLEDGE OF THE FUTURE

Doris Day once had a smash hit with the popular song, "Que Será, Será (Whatever Will Be, Will Be)." The words went like this:

When I was just a little girl,
I asked my mother, What will I be?
Will I be pretty? Will I be rich?
Here's what she said to me:

The mother's answer was vague. She had no crystal ball. All she could offer in response was the refrain: "*Que será, será*. Whatever will be, will be."

We worry about the future precisely because we do not know what it holds for us. The only reliable source for absolute knowledge of the future comes from the Lord of the future. Where God speaks of the future, we have sound reason for hope. Where He is silent, we are to desist from inquiry. The Old Testament abounds with severe prohibitions coupled with severe penalties for those who seek to see beyond the veil of time by illegitimate means.

But the ultimate question of our future plagues every human soul. Job asked the question this way: "If a man dies, shall he live again?" (Job 14:14).

Since death intruded into Paradise, the question of life after death has been paramount. Virtually every human culture has developed some form of hope in life beyond the grave. The ancient Egyptians placed precious items in the tombs of their deceased loved ones in that hope that these items would be useful in the afterlife. The American Indians had their concept of a happy hunting ground while the Norse had their hopes of Valhalla. The Jews had their shadowy concept of Sheol and the Greeks their view of Hades in the Stygian darkness.

Eastern religion responds with a view of reincarnation made popular by Shirley MacLaine and others. This idea, in various forms, has been posited from the time of Plato.

GREEK ARGUMENTS FOR LIFE AFTER DEATH

In the ancient world, Plato (428–348 B.C.) came under the influence of a group of philosophers called the Pythagoreans. The Pythagoreans are famous for the mystical significance they attached to numbers. The founder of the school, Pythagoras, developed the famous Pythagorean theorem that occupies a place in modern geometry. The Pythagoreans also conceived of the idea of the "transmigration of the soul," or reincarnation.

Their theory rested on the Greek premise that the human soul is immortal and eternal. In fact, the soul preexists the body. When a person is born, an eternal soul is temporarily "trapped" within a body. The body is a kind of prison house for the soul. The physical body, or prison, undergoes the process of generation and decay. When the body finally dies, the soul is released from its prison. In various views of reincarnation, the soul is then incarnated once more in a new body. Also, the soul migrates. It might be reincarnated in a higher form of life or a lower one. Usually the next migration or incarnation is dictated by the level of virtue achieved in the most recent incarnation. Ultimate redemption occurs when the soul finally breaks free of the cycle of incarnation and continues as a disembodied spirit, free of the inhibiting influence of the physical body. Plato basically accepted these premises, adding further insights of his own.

Plato set forth his speculations about life after death in his famous *Phaedo* dialogue. The scene takes place in an Athenian prison cell, where Socrates awaits execution for his "crime" of corrupting the youth of Athens by his penetrating and disturbing philosophical inquiries. We meet Socrates in his final hours as he awaits the guard who will bring him a fatal draught of hemlock. Socrates is surrounded by his friends and students. (Plato is absent because of illness.) There is a stark contrast in mood between the cheery disposition of Socrates and the frightened apprehension of his friends, who have already entered into mourning.

Socrates spends his final hours teaching his students about the anticipated joys of life after death. He says to his friends: "My words, too, are only an echo; but there is no reason why I should not repeat what I have heard: and indeed, as I am going to another place, it is very meet for me to be thinking and talking of the nature of the pilgrimage which I am about to make. What can I do better in the interval between this and the setting of the sun?"[1]

Socrates then declares his confidence in a future life by initiating a lengthy discussion on the theme: "And now, O my judges, I desire to prove to you that the real philosopher has reason to be of good cheer when he is about to die, and that after death he may hope to obtain the greatest good in the other world."[2]

What follows is an elaborate and complex "proof" for the immortality of the soul. Socrates gives an argument from opposites. He speculates about a universal opposition of all things—that there is a process we observe daily in nature by which things are generated by their opposites. Sleep proceeds to wakefulness, which in turn proceeds inexorably to sleep. Something that becomes greater can only become greater after first being less. That which undergoes diminution (becoming less) can only do so after first being greater.

In like manner, only that which is first alive can ever die. Life produces its opposite—death. So death must produce its opposite, which is life.

Socrates then attempts to prove that the souls of people existed before they were born. This argument rests on Plato's famous theory of recollection. In the recollection theory, Plato sought to prove (in this and other dialogues, especially in *Meno*) that we are born with certain ideas in our minds that can have come only from a preexistent state of the soul. Our ideas of beauty, goodness, justice, and holiness, for example, are not acquired from experience in this life but are already present at birth. The whole process we call "learning" is, in reality, merely a kind of stimulation of the memory to recall those ideas we understood more clearly in our souls before the negative influence of bodily passions dimmed them at birth.

Once Socrates proves this idea of recollection, and with it the preexistence of the soul, it is an easy step to presume the continuing existence of the soul after the body dies.

One of Socrates' students, Cebes, remains skeptical. He says to his mentor: "Then, Socrates, you must argue us out of our fears—and yet, strictly speaking, they are not our fears, but there is a child within us to whom death is a sort of hobgoblin: him too we must persuade not to be afraid when he is alone in the dark."[3]

Socrates proceeds to argue that the soul is a spiritual essence. He notes that as a spiritual essence, the soul is not made of matter, which is capable of decay or dissolution. Thus, it *cannot* die. Here is Socrates' reply: "Then reflect, Cebes: of all which has been said is not this the conclusion?—that the soul is in the very likeness of the divine, and immortal, and intellectual, and uniform, and indissoluble, and unchangeable; and that the body is in the very likeness of the human, and the mortal, and unintellectual, and multiform, and dissoluble, and changeable. Can this, my dear Cebes, be denied?"[4]

THE PROBLEM OF CORRUPTION

But there is a glitch in Socrates' reasoning. After he labors the point that the soul is unchangeable, he proceeds to declare that the soul is indeed changeable at one point. It is capable of moral corruption. He speaks of the pollution of the soul that must be cleansed through further incarnations: "What I mean is that men who have followed after gluttony, and wantonness, and drunkenness, and have had no thought of avoiding them, would pass into asses and animals of that sort."[5]

Socrates' speculation about reincarnation sounds a bit amusing to the modern reader (Shirley MacLaine notwithstanding). He speaks of men becoming wolves, hawks, bees, or wasps. (It would seem that we ought to be a bit solicitous toward garden spiders lest we trample on our great-great-grandfathers.)

The modern revival of interest in reincarnation raises some fascinating questions. Why do so many people find the idea of reincarnation so appealing? A simple answer may be that reincarnation seems to offer us a second chance at life.

We tend to wonder how things would be if we had the opportunity to live our lives over again. We wonder what changes we would make. Our dreams are tormented by the "what ifs" and the "might have beens" of life. We all carry a certain burden of unresolved guilt. A second trip through life offers the opportunity to atone for our sins, to make up for the failures and deficiencies of this life. The idea of repeated incarnations carries the hope of progress, the hope of rising higher and higher in our aspirations or our moral performance.

Yet reincarnation faces a massive difficulty that is rarely discussed among those who cling to this belief. It is the problem of continuity of conscious awareness.

I am a conscious human being. That consciousness includes a wonderful thing called memory. I remember experiences I had as a child. My memory bank stores a kind of knowledge of my personal history. Of course, some of these memories are unpleasant, while others are delightful. I am my personal history. I am not simply what I happen to do, think, or feel at this moment. I am the same human personality that opened toys on Christmas morning in 1943. Certainly there have been changes in my body, my thinking, my *self* since 1943. These changes continue as life continues. But there is a continuity of personality from the child of 1943 to the adult of the present.

Now suppose that this life is my third or fourth or hundredth incarnation. How much do I remember of my previous incarnations? In my case, the answer is simple: nothing. I have absolutely no recollection of any life experience prior to my birth. I realize that some people have tried to prove via hypnosis and other measures that they do possess some deeply buried vague memory of a previous life. These arguments appear to have more to do with imagination than genuine memory.

Do you remember living in this world before you were born? If not, then the dilemma is clear. Of what possible value is reincarnation if there is no conscious link between lives? If there is no continuity of consciousness, no memory whatever, how can we speak of personal continuity? If I continue to live after this life with no link of personal consciousness, will what follows really be me?

This entire speculation, which may seem bizarre to some readers, is rooted in a profoundly important matter. Beneath the level of the argument lurks the problem of the polluted soul and the question of unresolved justice.

There is a concern among sensitive people that this world does not always carry out perfect justice. We all observe that too often the righteous suffer and the wicked prosper. The world is long on tooth, fang, and claw, and, contrary to Hollywood, the underdog loses more often than he wins.

The haunting question remains: Why should I engage in acts of charity and sacrifice if life does not guarantee justice? Indeed, the whole question of ethical conduct becomes a quagmire of uncertainty. As Russian novelist Fyodor Dostoevsky wrote in his novel *The Brothers Karamazov*, "If there is no God, all things are permissible." Here he put his finger on the central issue— if there is no God, then there is no guarantee of ultimate justice. If there is no guarantee of ultimate justice, why should anyone ever act out of moral obligation? Why not just act out of pure self-interest?

THE NEED FOR AN "OUGHT" IN THE WORLD

In our daily lives, we cannot speak for very long without using words like *ought*, *should*, and *must*. We tell our children, "You ought to tell the truth." They may reply, "Why?" What do we say? We can rely on pure power tactics by replying, "Because I say so." We might appeal to their self-interest by saying, "Because honesty is the best policy." But even a child wonders whether honesty is the best policy if he has just taken cookies out of the cookie jar.

Anytime someone says, "You ought," we might be tempted to respond with one of two common questions: "Says who?" or "Why should I?" These questions raise the issue of the basis or ground of moral obligation. Is there any compelling reason why anyone can ever say "ought" about anything?

In the English language, there is a crucial difference between the statement, "I *want* to do something," and the statement, "I *ought* to do something." It is the difference between *desire* and *duty*. If I desire to do what my duty requires, there is no conflict. If I want to do what I ought to do, my decisions are easy. Moral struggle enters the picture when there is a conflict between desire and duty. It is when I want to do what I ought not to do or I do not want to do what I ought to do that I feel the pangs of a disturbed conscience.

The term *ought* is used more than one way. German philosopher Immanuel Kant made a distinction between two types of "oughtness" or imperatives. He distinguished between a "hypothetical imperative" and a "moral imperative."

A hypothetical imperative refers to a kind of oughtness that involves following certain means that are necessary to achieve certain desired ends. For example, if I go to work on a day that promises showers, I may say to myself, "I *ought* to take my umbrella." Here I am not speaking about a moral duty. (Unless, of course, I imply a moral obligation to take care of my body.) Rather, what I have in view is this: if I want to stay dry, I must avail myself of the necessary means to achieve that end. I must have an umbrella to shield myself from the rain. If I want to stay dry, then I must carry my umbrella.

Consider another illustration. Suppose a person decides to become a burglar. He desires to become a successful burglar. He reasons like this: "If I want to be a successful burglar, I *ought* to take precautions to make sure that I am not caught in the act of stealing." Here the burglar is thinking in terms of a hypothetical imperative. If he were thinking in terms of a moral imperative, he would be saying to himself, "I ought not be stealing at all."

As soon as we move from the hypothetical to the moral, we enter the arena of duty. Duty involves the matter of ethics. Here the word *ought* indicates a moral obligation. It means that what I want to do must be subordinated to what I ought to do.

We all experience the conflict between desire and duty. We all know that there are things we desire to do that are not right. At least we feel the weight of such conflict. But suppose there is no such thing as a morally right thing to do. Suppose that right and wrong are mere social conventions, arbitrary rules that help society run smoothly. Suppose that all imperatives are merely hypothetical imperatives that never pass over into moral imperatives. Then all that matters is for burglars to protect themselves from being caught. The only evil a burglar can do is to fail in his attempt to pull off a successful burglary.

What does all this have to do with life after death? In a word, everything.

If there is no such thing as right and wrong, if there is no such thing as *moral* obligation, then there is no such thing as justness. If there is no such thing as justness, then ultimately there is no such thing as justice. Justice becomes a mere sentiment. It means the preferences of an individual or a group. If the majority in one society prefers that adultery be rewarded, then justice is served when an adulterer receives a prize for his adultery. If the majority in a different society prefers that adultery be punished, then justice is served if the adulterer is penalized. But in this schema, there is no such thing as ultimate justice because the will of an individual or of a group can never serve as an ultimate moral norm for justice. It can reveal only a preference.

On the other hand, if there is such a thing as right and wrong, then we can talk about real justness. Then justice can be defined in terms of rewards and punishments distributed according to what is just. Then the term *ought* is packed with the power of real moral imperative.

Kant and Dostoevsky wrestled with this question: Without ultimate justice, can there ever be a sound basis for moral duty? If there is no ultimate justice, then why be concerned with being just? If we push this a bit, we can say that if my moral decisions do not count, then *I* do not count. If my actions do not count ultimately, then my life does not count ultimately.

That is why Kant saw that life without moral obligation is life without meaning. Oh, to be sure, we can *assign* meaning to our lives based on personal preferences and sentiments. But that is all we have, a sentimental wish that our lives have meaning. It is a sentimental wish that has both feet firmly planted in midair.

Kant recognized the universal reality of man's sense of right and wrong. Everyone functions with some sense of moral duty. We all feel the weight of the imperative "I ought." Kant then asked the practical question: "What is practically necessary for this moral sense to be meaningful?"

His first conclusion was crucial. He argued that for the moral sense of duty to be meaningful, there must be such a thing as justness. For justness, or right and wrong, to be meaningful, there must be justice. Thus, justice serves as a necessary condition for moral obligation to be meaningful.

Ah, but here's the rub: in this world, justice is not always done. Too many burglars are successful in their endeavors. Does this mean that crime ultimately does pay and that there is no vindication for the just person?

That is the only conclusion we could reach if there were no ultimate justice. There might be "proximate justice," that is, partial and occasional justice where the burglar was caught and his victims' possessions returned intact, but still the scales of justice would too often be out of balance. For justness to have any ultimate meaning, we need more than proximate justice; we need ultimate justice.

If ultimate justice is to be had, the first requirement that must be met is this: we must survive the grave. If we do not survive the grave, and if justice is not served perfectly in this world, then justice is not ultimate and our sense of moral obligation is a meaningless striving after the wind.

If ultimate justice is served, we must be there to experience it. Unless we survive the grave, we cannot have justice. Here Kant is echoing the thoughts of Socrates and Plato, in addition to the thoughts of Job and Ecclesiastes.

THE NEED FOR THE PERFECT JUDGE

But suppose we *do* survive the grave. Suppose we return in another incarnation as a wasp or a donkey. We still may be haunted by further injustice. Like Balaam's ass, we might have a master who beats us without just cause. Or we might fly as a wasp into some unjust fellow's burst of Raid.

We cannot have a trial without a person who is being tried. But neither can there be a trial if the only person present is the accused. There must be a judge. No judge, no judgment. No judgment, no justice.

Therefore, a second necessary condition for ultimate justice is the presence of an ultimate judge. But no ordinary judge will do. For ultimate justice to be insured, the judge must have the proper characteristics.

First of all, the judge himself must be perfectly just. If there is a moral blemish in the judge's character, then chances are his judgments will be tainted and our quest for perfect justice will fail.

Suppose the judge were totally just but had other shortcomings. Suppose he had the best intentions and was morally impeccable, but lacked the necessary knowledge to render a perfect verdict. We can conceive of a judge who himself is beyond reproach, neither given to bribes or to prejudice, but who doesn't grasp all the nuances of complex sets of mitigating circumstances. He could render a verdict to the best of his ability, but it still might not be perfectly just. Perfect justice requires a perfect knowledge of every conceivable mitigating circumstance. It is possible that perfect justice could happen apart from perfect knowledge, but it would be by a fortunate accident. For perfect justice to be insured, the perfect judge must have perfect knowledge. In a word, the perfect judge must be omniscient lest some relevant detail escape his notice and distort his verdict.

But suppose our perfect judge acts with perfect integrity and with perfect knowledge and renders a perfect verdict. Is that enough to insure perfect justice? No, not yet. If a perfect decision is rendered, it still must be carried out. Perfect laws do not guarantee perfect behavior. Perfect verdicts do not insure perfect consequences. The prisoner may escape from jail and cheat justice.

For perfect justice to be carried out, the judge must have the power necessary to see that justice is truly served. He must have enough power to withstand any attempt to disrupt the flow of justice. There cannot be a single maverick molecule outside the scope of his power and authority, lest that single molecule become the grain of sand that brings the machine of justice to a grinding halt. Therefore, the perfect judge must have perfect power. He must be all-powerful, or omnipotent.

There is good news in the biblical assertion that "The Lord God Omnipotent reigneth" (Rev. 19:6). If the Lord God Omnipotent does not reign, we have no hope of justice. A Lord God Impotent cannot serve the cause of justice. Nothing less than a morally perfect, omniscient, immutable, eternal, and omnipotent God can insure that our moral sense of obligation is meaningful. No God, no justice. No justice, no ultimate right and wrong.

That brings us back to Dostoevsky's conclusion: if there is no God, then all things are permissible. Such a conclusion leaves man and society no real grounds for ethics. Without an ethical base, society becomes impossible to maintain. It may last for the short haul while it is tenuously held together by the remains of theistic norms. But ultimately it will fail by the sheer weight of its intolerable conventions.

Therefore, Kant argued for the existence of God and for life after death on practical grounds. He maintained that we must make these two assumptions if justice is to have any basis.

Kant realized that such practical considerations do not "prove" the existence of God. He was saying only that if life is to be meaningful, there must be a God who ensures justice. These considerations prove only that if my sense of right and wrong are meaningful, then God must exist. Kant said, "We must live as if there is a God."

The advantage of Kant's argument is not that it proves the existence of God or life after death. The advantage is that it cuts off the heads of all the philosophies that want to have their cake and eat it, too. It smashes all the middle-ground views that want to find a resting place somewhere between full-fledged theism and radical nihilism.

It is not by accident that many philosophers since Kant have turned to nihilistic philosophies of despair. They argue that we cannot believe in God or life after death simply because the alternatives to these beliefs are so grim. They say: "Let's face the music: there is no God and no justice. There is no such thing as right and wrong. We live alone in a universe that is neither hostile nor hospitable toward our moral decisions." No, it is far worse than that. We live in a universe that is ultimately *indifferent* to human actions. It ultimately doesn't care about man because man ultimately has no worth.

Every bone in our bodies protests against such a negative view of human life. Every breath we draw is breathed with the hope that our lives do matter. It is intolerable to our minds that all is futile. We take comfort in the practical speculations of philosophers like Socrates and Kant, but we long for more. We need assurance beyond the mere practical wish that justice be done.

What we need is a word from "out there." We need some tangible evidence that our hope is not a mere illusion based on our inner drive for meaning and significance. We need more than an "as if" to bring us courage.

This is why the "news" of the New Testament is so vital. Here we possess a record that goes beyond speculation to historical reality. Let us turn then to the message and the record of the Christ. Let us hear the message of Jesus of Nazareth and the testimony to His conquest over the grave.

Notes

1   *The Works of Plato*, ed. Irwin Edman (New York: Random House, 1956), 114.
2   Ibid., 117.
3   Ibid., 137.
4   Ibid., 140.
5   Ibid., 143.

CHAPTER EIGHT

JESUS AND THE AFTERLIFE

To rise above the speculation of philosophers and bypass the occult, we must turn our attention to Jesus. No one's teaching on the subject of life after death equals or surpasses that of Jesus of Nazareth. The concept of life beyond the grave was at the core of His message.

One of the best-known words of Jesus on the subject of life after death is found in John 14. Here Jesus was present in the upper room for the Last Supper. The discussion recorded here took place on the eve of Christ's crucifixion, shortly before His agony in Gethsemane and His subsequent arrest.

To comfort His friends, Jesus declared the following: "Let not your heart be troubled; you believe in God, believe also in Me. In My Father's house are many mansions; if it were not so, I would have told you. I go to prepare a place for you. And if I go and prepare a place for you, I will come again and receive you to Myself; that where I am, there you may be also" (John 14:1–3).

Why were the disciples gripped by troubled hearts? We know that Jesus Himself was "troubled in spirit" that evening (John 13:21). He was troubled by the announcement He was about to make of His imminent betrayal at the hands of Judas.

Imagine the setting. A pall of foreboding gloom hangs over the upper room. Three years of public ministry, three years of close fellowship among His disciples, had brought them to this hour. It was an hour of profound crisis. There was much to be troubled about. A sense of finality hovered about them. Jesus knew that His hour had come. He revealed His impending death to His friends. He added to their apprehension by announcing three very troubling things. He declared that Judas was going to betray Him, that Peter was going to deny Him, and, worst of all, that He was going to leave them physically. He said: "Little children, I shall be with you a little while longer. You will seek Me; and as I said to the Jews, 'Where I am going you cannot come,' so now I say to you" (John 13:33).

Here Peter exclaimed, "Lord, where are You going?" Jesus replied, "Where I am going you cannot follow Me now, but you shall follow Me afterward" (13:36).

These words of Christ are packed with historical content. Jesus' relationship with Simon Peter began with two simple words, "Follow Me" (Matt. 4:19). Peter walked away from his nets and followed Jesus. Wherever Jesus went, Peter went. He was with Jesus at the wedding feast of Cana. He was with Jesus on the Mount of Transfiguration. He even followed Jesus by walking on the water. Now the time of following was abruptly over. Jesus said, "You cannot follow Me now."

One of the most difficult struggles a person experiences as he approaches death is the troubling knowledge that the journey must be made alone, without human companionship. We can sit by the bedside of our loved ones. We can hold their hands and they can hold ours. But a moment comes when separation takes place. It is that separation, however temporary, that distresses our spirits. Often at the precise moment of death, when the last breath is taken and the heartbeat falls silent, the announcement is made, "He's gone!" For this reason, we describe death as a departure, a separation.

When Elijah was being cared for by the widow of Zarephath, the widow's son became seriously ill and died. The Old Testament records that Elijah raised the son from the dead. But before the miracle took place, the woman berated Elijah in her distress. She cried out to him: "What have I to do with you, O man of God? Have you come to me to bring my sin to remembrance, and to kill my son?" (1 Kings 17:18).

Elijah responded with a command: "Give me your son." Then Scripture says that Elijah took him out of her arms and carried him to the upper room where he was staying (17:19).

Before Elijah performed the miracle, he had to take the dead boy out of his mother's arms. It is obvious from the text that in her grief the woman was desperately hanging on to the corpse of her child. Elijah had to pry them apart.

The scene is not uncommon. We want to hold on to our loved ones as long as possible. The moment of separation is almost unbearable.

Even Jesus' postscript is enigmatic. What did He mean about Peter following Him afterward? Peter probably understood these words to mean, "You cannot follow Me in death now, but afterwards you shall also die."

The question then is this: Where was Peter to follow? Was He merely to follow Jesus to the grave? No. Jesus answered these questions in John 14. When He said, "Let not your heart be troubled," He gave a reason for His command.

First, He called the disciples to an act of faith. He said, "You believe in God, believe also in Me" (John 14:1). He was saying simply, "Trust Me." Jesus does not ask for a leap of blind faith. When He asked His disciples to trust Him, there was a backlog of history to support His request. It was as if Jesus were saying: "Look, I've never let you down. My Father has never broken a promise. I haven't either. I have proven Myself to be trustworthy. Now, when I go away, it's time to trust Me on the force of My promise. You believe in God, now believe in Me. The key to putting your troubled hearts to rest is to trust Me for the future."

This is the heart of Christianity. This is why we speak of the Christian *faith*, not the Christian *religion*. Religion has to do with the outward cultic practices of human beings. Christianity, the Christian faith, has to do with trusting God for our very lives. The step Jesus asked His disciples to take was a big step. It is one thing to believe *in* God; it is quite another to *believe* God. This is a major step in practice, though in theory it should not require any step at all. Our distinction between believing in God and believing God should be a distinction without a difference, a sheer exercise in sophistry. In truth, if we really believe in God, we will believe whatever God tells us.

Yet in terms of concrete reality, there is often a gap between our theoretical faith in God and our actual trust in what He says. Our faith is not pure. Like gold that is marred by dross, so our faith is often mixed with doubt. We cry out, "Lord, I believe; help my unbelief!" (Mark 9:24).

At the moment of death, fear and doubt can assault the heart and press hard against our faith. It is at that moment that we must hear the words of Jesus: "Trust Me."

PREPARING A PLACE IN THE FATHER'S HOUSE

Jesus went on to declare the substance of the "where" that the disciples would ultimately follow: "In My Father's house are many mansions. . . . I go to prepare a place for you" (John 14:2).

At age twelve, Jesus had confounded the theologians in the temple. When His anxious parents found Him there, His mother scolded Him: "Son, why have You done this to us? Look, Your father and I have sought You anxiously" (Luke 2:48).

The boy Jesus replied with a thinly veiled rebuke of His anxiety-stricken mother: "Why did you seek Me? Did you not know that I must be about My Father's business?" (2:49).

The Father's business took place in the temple. Later Jesus referred to the temple in Jerusalem as His Father's house, saying, "Do not make My Father's house a house of merchandise!" (John 2:16).

In John 14, Jesus again spoke of His Father's house. He was no longer referring to the temple in Jerusalem. The temple was the earthly, Old Testament house of God. That house was perishable and indeed was destroyed in AD 70. Instead, Jesus was speaking of heaven, the ultimate residence of His Father.

Jesus promised His disciples that they would follow Him one day to the Father's house in heaven. He declared, "I go to prepare a place for you." Jesus explained that His departure from their midst, which was troubling their hearts, should be an occasion of great joy. Jesus left them to go to prepare their rooms in heaven.

Jesus not only made it possible for us to go to heaven, He has actually gone there to assure our reservations and prepare our rooms for us.

I spend months of the year away from my home. Doing so much traveling has had a long-term impact on me. Over the years, I noticed several patterns emerging in my own psyche about traveling. For one thing, I became more fussy about reservations. There are few things more frustrating for a weary traveler than to arrive at his destination and discover that the hotel has failed to record his reservation or has given his room to somebody else. These mix-ups do occur and are maddening when they happen.

On our trip to heaven, we have the best of all possible reservations, prepared by the best of all possible advance men. Jesus Himself has gone before us to prepare a place in our Father's house. No mix-up can happen with these reservations.

If we belong to Christ, we have a rock-solid reservation. There are many rooms in the Father's house. There is a place for us that no one else can take away.

AN "ADULT" VIEW OF ETERNAL LIFE

I think that the most comforting words Jesus ever spoke about heaven are found in John 14:2. Jesus said, "If it were not so, I would have told you."

The tone of this utterance has a paternal ring to it. Jesus was speaking as a Father speaks to his children. We note that moments earlier Jesus had addressed His disciples as "little children," saying, "Little children, I shall be with you a little while longer" (John 13:33). There comes a time in children's lives when parents must tell them how things really are. Infants must be weaned away from the realm of fairy tales and myths. The day of sober truth arrives when a child becomes too old to maintain a belief in Santa Claus and the Easter Bunny. A transaction takes place that involves the demythologizing of life. The fun and enchantment of childhood must give way to the realities of adulthood. There is a time when childish things must be put away. The apostle Paul declared: "When I was a child, I spoke as a child, I understood as a child, I thought as a child; but when I became a man, I put away childish things" (1 Cor. 13:11).

If a man fails to put away childish things, he faces adulthood severely handicapped. To hang on to childhood myths too long is to be crippled intellectually.

Jesus understood that if His disciples were going to be able to carry out their mission as adults, if they were going to be able to face the tribulations that were certainly going to be theirs, they had to be able to discern the difference between myth and reality.

As a teacher, Jesus, like any other teacher, had to help His pupils unlearn mistaken ideas they carried into His classroom. Education involves far more than acquiring new information. True education involves the often-painful process of discarding pet ideas and theories that will not hold up under critical scrutiny. Jesus' teaching involved correction of erroneous concepts.

However, when He spoke in the upper room, Jesus announced that one of the disciples' pet concepts was in no need of correction. The disciples' hope for life after death was not a myth or a fantasy. Their belief in eternal life was not based on a form of wish-projection. There was nothing childish about it.

Jesus declared, "If it were not so, I would have told you." This declaration was a negative form of divine revelation. Baleful existential theologians to the contrary, it may be received as propositional truth. The statement comes in the literary form of a conditional "if-then" statement. What is in view here is a simple condition contrary to fact.

Jesus was saying this: "If your faith in a future life was not valid, I would have corrected your false hopes. I would not have let so weighty a false idea go uncorrected. But the fact of the matter is that there is a heaven and you can count on it."

Here is a dogmatic utterance par excellence. Jesus spoke to this point not merely as a highly skilled and knowledgeable rabbi, or even as an anointed prophet of God. He spoke with the absolute and infallible authority of the Son of God. We recall that Jesus declared boldly that "All authority has been given to Me in heaven and on earth" (Matt. 28:18). Here He manifested that authority. If the One who possesses all authority in heaven speaks a word about heaven, it follows that His teaching on the subject is impeccable.

Therefore, if this boldest of all human claims was correct, then Jesus' statements provide the highest and most trustworthy source of information we could ever find on the subject of heaven.

THE MATTER OF JESUS' AUTHORITY

Jesus claimed to receive His authority from the source of all authority, indeed the Author of authority, God Himself. He added to this claim with other statements:

> "My doctrine is not Mine, but His who sent Me. . . . You both know Me, and you know where I am from; and I have not come of Myself, but He who sent Me is true, whom you do not know. But I know Him, for I am from Him, and He sent Me." (John 7:16, 28–29)

> "I have many things to say and to judge concerning you, but He who sent Me is true; and I speak to the world those things which I heard from Him. . . . I do nothing of Myself; but as My Father taught Me, I speak these things." (John 8:26–28)

John the Baptist echoed this claim when he bore witness to Jesus' authority by saying: "He who comes from above is above all; he who is of the earth is earthly and speaks of the earth. He who comes from heaven is above all. . . . For He whom God has sent speaks the words of God, for God does not give the Spirit by measure" (John 3:31–34).

When we receive important information, whether from the news media or from a scholarly textbook, we are urged to "consider the source." We seek documentation for any data to insure that the information is credible. The source Jesus claimed for His information was the same source He claimed for His authority, namely God Himself.

Jesus' contemporaries, including those who were hostile toward Him, were often confounded by His manner of speaking:

> And so it was, when Jesus had ended these sayings, that the people were astonished at His teaching, for He taught them as one having authority, and not as the scribes. (Matt. 7:28–29)

> Now some of them wanted to take Him, but no one laid hands on Him. Then the officers came to the chief priests and Pharisees, who said to them, "Why have you not brought Him?" The officers answered, "No man ever spoke like this Man!" (John 7:44–46)

Jesus spoke as one having authority. The Greek word that is used here for "authority" is *exousia*. The term *exousia* is made up of the prefix *ex*, meaning "from" or "out of," and the root *ousia*, which is the present participle of the verb "to be." Literally the word means "out of being" or "substance."

The term *exousia* is usually translated as "authority" or "power." There is an element of both ideas compressed within the word *exousia*. We can translate it as "powerful authority." It is an authority based on substance or being.

In simple terms, when the Bible says that Jesus spoke as One having authority, it simply means that Jesus was not uttering an empty or vaporous opinion. He had the "stuff" or the "substance" of reality behind His words. His authority was backed up by nothing less than the very being or substance of God.

When God speaks, all dispute about the truth and reality of what is spoken must end, except for those who are perpetually stubborn or incomprehensibly foolish. Who else would dare to correct the Deity?

If Jesus spoke the truth concerning His authority, then no objection can withstand the conclusion that He spoke the truth regarding life after death.

His declaration, "If it were not so, I would have told you," remains the consolation of all consolations.

THE ULTIMATE COMFORT FOR THE BEREAVED

The bringing of comfort to the bereaved is a task each of us faces from time to time. It is often an unenviable and intimidating task. A funeral parlor is a stage where the most accomplished speaker stutters. We feel woefully inadequate to the task of finding the right words to say to those in mourning.

I once visited the funeral parlor where the body of my first employer's wife was laid out for final viewing. Her husband had hired me as a shoeshine boy when I was fourteen. I worked alongside him in his cobbler's shop. Over the years, I kept in touch with him and counted him a friend.

When I visited the funeral home, I had no words of wisdom to offer. All I could think to do was to sit by his side quietly for an hour or so. All I had to offer him was my presence, an unspoken testimony to my care for him in his hour of grief. I remained silent on that occasion because I had no words to say that I thought were adequate to the need. My vocabulary failed me. I could not speak with *exousia* about anything.

When Jesus went to the home of Mary and Martha on the occasion of their brother Lazarus' death, He consoled them with words of *exousia*. He declared to Martha, "Your brother will rise again" (John 11:23).

Martha understood Jesus' words to refer to the future hope of resurrection: "I know that he will rise again in the resurrection at the last day" (John 11:24). To this Jesus replied: "I am the resurrection and the life. He who believes in Me, though he may die, he shall live. And whoever lives and believes in Me shall never die. Do you believe this?" (John 11:25–26).

Jesus of Nazareth never uttered a bolder statement than this. He directly linked eternal life with Himself. He tied everlasting life, ultimate victory over the greatest enemy of all mankind, death itself, with faith in Him. To believe in Christ is to gain eternal life.

Few people in the history of the world have dared to make such a claim. Only one backed up the claim with action.

Far beyond the words of Jesus stands the record of His deeds. His example matches the power of His words. Only moments after His words of comfort to Martha, Jesus went to the grave of Lazarus. Martha protested against the removal of the stone that sealed the entrance. Lazarus had been dead for four days. Presumably he had not been embalmed. Martha shrunk in horror at the expected stench of the corpse of her brother.

When the stone was removed, Jesus uttered a command in a loud voice. By divine imperative, He ordered Lazarus back from death: "Lazarus, come forth!"

Lazarus was bound hand and foot with grave clothes. Likewise, his soul had departed, so that he was bound tightly by the grip of death. However, at the command of Jesus, death released its grip. Lazarus' heart began to beat. Blood started to flow afresh in his veins. Decomposing tissue was instantly restored to vibrant health. Lazarus became conscious. He was suddenly mobile. Despite the constricting grave clothes, he walked out of his tomb. Jesus gave another command to those standing by: "Loose him, and let him go" (John 11:44).

What Jesus did for Lazarus, for Jairus' daughter (Luke 8:40–42, 49–56), and for the widow of Nain's son (Luke 7:11–15) was also accomplished in His own body.

On the day of His death, Jesus was taunted by mockers who cried, "He saved others; let Him save Himself if He is the Christ, the chosen of God" (Luke 23:35). Jesus knew that in His hour of death a legion of angels was available to rescue Him in a moment. A simple word from Christ would have been enough to mobilize the angelic forces in His behalf. But His duty was to die. He drank the cup, and with His final words He entrusted Himself to His Father.

For three days the Son of God was dead. For three days the Father was silent. For three days those who mocked Jesus felt triumph in their hostility toward Him. For three days His friends and disciples mourned their incomparable loss. For three days they hid in fear and bewilderment.

Then the Lord God Omnipotent broke the silence. He did not scream. There was no trumpet heralding. There was quietness in the garden, broken only by the soft weeping of Mary Magdalene. Mary was distressed by the discovery that Jesus' body was missing from the tomb. His corpse had disappeared in what seemed to her to be the final and most senseless assault against His dignity. Someone, she assumed, had stolen the body of Christ.

Someone was standing behind her. She thought it was the gardener. He spoke: "Woman, why are you weeping? Whom are you seeking?" (John 20:15). Mary replied, "Sir, if you have carried Him away, tell me where you have laid Him, and I will take Him away" (John 20:15b).

Then Mary heard the man speak her name: "Mary!" Instant recognition flooded her soul at the sound of His voice. She turned and exclaimed simply, "Rabboni!" which means "teacher."

Jesus had risen from the dead. "He is risen" was to become the first creed of Christendom.

The resurrection of Christ is the central affirmation of the Christian church. With its truth stands or falls the whole of the Christian religion. If there was no resurrection, there is no Christianity. If there was no resurrection, there is no reason to continue the church, save as one more social agency cloaking humanitarian services in mythical religious garb.

There have been numerous attempts to construct a Christianity without a bodily resurrection. In the nineteenth century, so-called liberal Christians tried to modernize the Christian faith by stripping it of its "nonessential" miraculous husk and reducing it to its ethical kernel. The supernatural elements were rejected in an attempt to offer a religion of values that would enhance life in this world without requiring adherents to get caught up in an otherworldly fixation on pie in the sky by and by. Jesus became for them the supreme model of brotherly love who demonstrated an altruistic self-sacrifice that ended with His heroic death. Jesus the divine Savior from death and the Victor over the grave became Jesus the human teacher of ethics.

Such a Jesus has no need of a church. Worship is at best a hollow service and at worst an act of blasphemy if it is directed toward a dead teacher of morality. We have no church for Socrates. We sing no hymns to Cicero. We say no prayers to Aristotle. If Jesus is a mere human teacher, neither should we worship Him.

PAUL'S ARGUMENT FOR RESURRECTION

Attempts to create a Christianity without a resurrection began early in the church's history. The apostle Paul had to confront the problem in the troublesome Corinthian church. The apostle's rebuke to the Corinthian congregation is as relevant today as it was when it was first given. It may be even more relevant now because what once was a local problem restricted to an isolated situation is an epidemic in the church of the twenty-first century.

The apostle addressed the Corinthians with a crucial question: "Now if Christ is preached that He has been raised from the dead, how do some among you say that there is no resurrection of the dead?" (1 Cor. 15:12).

Here we find members of the early Christian community who denied life after death. Their rejection was categorical and absolute. They insisted that there was no resurrection from the dead. No one, not even Jesus, survives the grave, they claimed.

Paul responded to this view by stepping on his opponents' toes to demonstrate the radical inconsistency and utter absurdity of a Christian faith without the bodily resurrection of Jesus Christ. Let us trace the apostle's argument point by point as he spells out the logical implications of no resurrection. He moves in a progressive manner, mounting a series of negative implications that follow an irresistible logic.

Point 1: "But if there is no resurrection of the dead, then Christ is not risen" (1 Cor. 15:13).

Who can argue with such logic? A universal negative proposition (no resurrection of the dead) allows for no exception. The laws of immediate inference do not allow a "none" coupled with a "some." Here we find a conditional proposition where the conclusion cannot be refuted. If A is true, then B must also be true. If there is no resurrection of the dead, then, manifestly, Christ is not risen.

Point 2: "If Christ is not risen, then our preaching is empty and your faith is also empty" (15:14).

Here Paul sets himself against all forms of liberalized Christianity that seek to deny the resurrection of Christ on the one hand and continue to preach and call people to "faith" on the other hand. In Paul's view, this is a foolish attempt to have one's cake and eat it too. He views this as an absurd exercise in futility. Without a real, bodily resurrection, Christian preaching is useless.

Paul does not commit the fallacy of a false dilemma here. He sees the issue as a genuine case of the either/or. Either Christ is raised or preaching and faith are useless.

Point 3: "Yes, and we are found false witnesses of God, because we have testified of God that He raised up Christ, whom He did not raise up—if in fact the dead do not rise" (15:15).

If ever the apostle ran the risk of insulting his readers by laboring the obvious, it is here. For Paul to add the last portion of this sentence ("whom He did not raise up—if in fact the dead do not rise") was to spell out the most obvious of conclusions. I sense a hint of sarcasm dripping from the apostle's pen here. Nothing could be simpler to understand then the conclusion that if the dead do not rise then God did not raise Christ.

But there is a more ominous note here. Paul was writing as a Jewish theologian. He was acutely aware of the seriousness of bearing false witness. To bear false witness against men is a capital offense proscribed in the Ten Commandments. To bear false witness against God is an even more serious offense.

Paul's reasoning was this: if Christ is not raised, then Paul and the other apostles must be judged as false prophets. They were members of Jehovah's False Witnesses. To deny the apostolic proclamation of the resurrection while at the same time extolling their virtues as teachers of ethics was to praise the folly of false prophets. The apostle himself saw this as a hopeless contradiction. He saw himself disqualified as a trusted teacher if his witness to the resurrection was false. Here Paul put his and the other apostles' total reputation and integrity on the line. It is as if Paul said, "Take me or leave me on this point."

Point 4: "And if Christ is not risen, your faith is futile; you are still in your sins!" (15:17).

Again the apostle pressed the point of futility. Without resurrection, the

Christian faith is futile. It is useless, a waste of time, energy, and devotion. To believe in a false hope is to set the heart on a course for ultimate frustration. Without the resurrection, we are left with no hope. All we have to show for our pilgrimage is unresolved guilt.

Paul saw the resurrection as God's clear sign of His acceptance of Christ's sacrifice as an atonement for our sins (Rom. 1:4). Therefore, if He was not raised, we remain in our sins. We have no Savior. Both our faith and Christ's death are equally useless. We remain debtors who cannot pay our debts.

Point 5: "Then also those who have fallen asleep in Christ have perished" (15:18).

Of the negative implications of no resurrection, this is perhaps the most grim of all. Paul did not shrink from the brutal conclusion: no resurrection means that death brings the end of all hope. In his *Divine Comedy*, Dante Alighieri imagined a sign posted on the doorway of hell: "Abandon hope all ye who enter here." Paul placed that sign right here, right now. It is posted not at the gate of hell but at the door of every funeral home.

Every person who has lost a loved one to death knows the poignant hope that abides. It is the hope that somewhere, sometime, we will see our loved ones again. That hope is the consolation we cling to when death separates us from our loved ones.

On one awful occasion, I sat with my daughter and her husband in the delivery room of a hospital maternity ward. My daughter had just given birth to a little girl. The baby was stillborn. In cases like that, it was the policy of the hospital to allow the mother and father to hold the dead infant for a while. Pictures were taken. The baby's footprints were recorded in ink. The baby was named and a record was made of the weight and length of the child. A lock of hair was attached to the record sheet. The certificate with its data was given to the parents when the child was removed to be prepared for burial. The paper was called a "certificate of remembrance."

My daughter came home from the hospital with photos and a certificate of remembrance. She also came home with the profound hope that someday she will see her daughter again, alive.

Yet, Paul reasons, if Christ is not raised, those who have died have perished forever. It is the fate of all men to recite the mournful refrain of Edgar Allan Poe's "The Raven": "Nevermore."

Point 6: "Otherwise, what will they do who are baptized for the dead, if the dead do not rise at all? Why then are they baptized for the dead?" (15:29).

Paul continued by showing the radical inconsistency of those who practiced baptism for the dead in Corinth. This passing mention of baptism for the dead is the only New Testament reference to such a practice. It has evoked all kinds of consternation. Paul neither commended nor condemned the practice. He merely acknowledged that it was practiced among the Corinthians and showed the absurdity of it if there is no resurrection. To baptize the dead if there is no resurrection would be a waste of time and a waste of water.

Point 7: "And why do we stand in jeopardy every hour? I affirm, by the boasting in you which I have in Christ Jesus our Lord, I die daily. If, in the manner of men, I have fought with beasts at Ephesus, what advantage is it to me?" (15:30–32).

Here we find a fascinating application. The apostle turned to his own ministry as evidence of his conviction that the resurrection "made sense" of his own trials. He affirmed his position by taking an oath on his ministry in Christ. Such oath-taking was not a casual matter for a pious Jew. He testified that his own ministry would be worthless apart from the resurrection. For a summary of the herculean pain and effort that marked Paul's ministry, the reader might take a few moments to peruse 2 Corinthians 11, where Paul gave a brief record of his suffering in the ministry.

A popular argument for the resurrection goes something like this: Which is more difficult to believe, that Christ rose from the dead or that the apostles were willing to die for a hoax?

I've never found such arguments very satisfying. On the surface, we must admit that though it is rare to find fanatics who are so deluded that they are willing to die for something that is not true, or even for something they know is not true, it is not as rare as a resurrection from the dead.

An appeal to Paul's extraordinary devotion to his ministry and his willingness to die for his faith does not prove conclusively that his faith was valid.

What it does show, however, is that his behavior was consistent with what we might expect from someone who was an eyewitness of the resurrected Jesus. What was true of Paul was true of the other apostles as well. They lived and died in the full confidence of the resurrection of Christ.

Point 8: "If the dead do not rise, 'Let us eat and drink, for tomorrow we die!'" (15:32).

Here Paul cut through all the trappings of religious sentimentality and altruism. He echoed the creed of the ancient Epicurean. If there is no life after death, the only sensible lifestyle is that of the blatant hedonist. We might as well grab all the pleasure we can before we are swallowed by final pain. Here is the apostolic anticipation of modern skepticism: grab all the gusto you can because "You only go around once"; or, alternatively, "Whoever dies with the most toys, wins."

Point 9: "If in this life only we have hope in Christ, we are of all men the most pitiable" (15:19).

Though it comes earlier in Paul's argument, I saved this point for last. Paul could hardly have protested louder against all attempts to construct a Christian religion without the bodily resurrection of Jesus Christ. If the value of Christian hope is restricted to this life, then Christians are the most miserable of all people. Their misery is this: they live a life based on false hope. That hope is a controlling hope. It involves an ethic of postponed reward, an ethic of present sacrifice for the sake of future reward.

Paul was saying that if you are hostile toward Christians, you really should exchange your hostility for pity. Christians who live with deluded hope need pity. They need pity because they are indeed the most pitiable of all people.

THE BASIS OF EYEWITNESSES

The most important dimension of Paul's argument for the resurrection is this: it does not rest simply on a speculative basis of grim options. Paul was not concluding that since life without resurrection is miserable we should therefore take a deep breath, close our eyes, and conjure up faith in a resurrection. Paul did not say we must live *as if* there were a resurrection because without it all these devastatingly hopeless conclusions must be faced. His nine-point argument was merely corroborative. It was a study in consistency. It was not the basis of his confidence in the resurrection of Christ.

Paul's case for the resurrection went far beyond speculative philosophy. He provided evidence that neither Plato nor Kant could offer. He appealed to eyewitness testimony to the historical reality of Jesus' resurrection:

> For I delivered to you first of all that which I also received; that Christ died for our sins according to the Scriptures, and that He was buried, and that He rose again the third day according to the Scriptures, and that He was seen by Cephas, then by the twelve. After that He was seen by over five hundred brethren at once, of whom the greater part remain to the present, but some have fallen asleep. After that He was seen by James, then by all the apostles. Then last of all He was seen by me also, as by one born out of due time. (1 Cor. 15:3-8)

This is the record of history concerning Jesus of Nazareth. His life, His death, His burial, and His resurrection were all foretold by Scripture. Testimony to His resurrection was not based on inferences or conclusions drawn from the appearance of an empty tomb. A missing corpse was not enough. The testimony was based on the appearances of Jesus alive, and not to one or two people, but to a host of people.

Paul named the people who saw Jesus return from the grave alive. This list includes some who witnessed the crucifixion and the final spear thrust in Jesus' side. It includes people who saw the corpse prepared for burial.

The eyewitnesses included one group that numbered more than five hundred people on a single occasion. Furthermore, Paul claimed that most of the eyewitnesses were still alive. It was as if he said: "Check it out. The witnesses can still be cross-examined."

We do not have the opportunity now to cross-examine the five hundred. But we still have the written record of the apostolic eyewitnesses. We still can read John's account or Matthew's.

Finally Paul declared that he personally saw the resurrected Christ. Paul's words are thrilling. Topping all secondhand reports, the apostle declared: "He was seen by me also."

Paul said, "I saw Him!" That's what Plato and Kant could never say.

It is no wonder that Paul exuded confidence in the victory of Christ over death. His final conclusion followed irresistibly from his stirring testimony: "Therefore, my beloved brethren, be steadfast, immovable, always abounding in the work of the Lord, knowing that your labor is not in vain in the Lord" (1 Cor. 15:58).

Paul's "therefore" signals the grand conclusion. There is solid ground for this solemn admonition: be steadfast. With the certainty of resurrection, steadfastness is called for. Vacillation is not the mark of those who know the resurrected Christ. The resurrection provides the anchor for the soul that makes it an immovable object. Furthermore, believers should be always abounding in the work of the Lord. The resurrection sparks work in abundance. It is labor that rests in the certainty that no effort made in Christ is futile. Our labor, our pain, our suffering—yea, even our dying—are never in vain.

CHAPTER NINE

TO DIE IS GAIN

Blaise Pascal once observed that a crucial element of man's misery is found in this—he can always contemplate a better life than it is possible for him to achieve. This is because we all have the ability to dream, to allow our imaginations to soar in flights of fancy.

However, when we push our imaginative powers to their limit and attempt to envision the best life possible, we crash into the barrier of the unknown. Who can imagine what heaven is really like? It is beyond our comprehension. It is beyond our most ambitious dreams.

One sage remarked that if we were to imagine the most pleasant experience possible and thought about doing that for eternity, we would be conceiving of something that would be closer to hell than to heaven. We simply cannot fathom a situation of absolute felicity. We have no concrete reference point for it.

It is the mysterious, uncharted nature of the afterlife that provoked Hamlet to declare:

Who would fardels bear,
To grunt and sweat under a weary life,

But that the dread of something after death,
The undiscovered country, from whose bourn
No traveler returns, puzzles the will,
And makes us rather bear those ills we have
Than fly to others that we know not of?
Thus conscience does make cowards of us all.
(*Hamlet*, Act III, Scene I)

Perhaps Hamlet had a sense of the flip side of Pascal's observation. Not only do we have the ability to contemplate a better existence than we presently enjoy, we also have the power to imagine a worse existence than we presently endure. It is the unknown quality of the afterlife that makes us bear the ills we have rather than fly to others we know not of.

Our imaginings about the afterlife are restricted primarily to analogy. To move beyond this world is to move into another dimension. That different dimension involves both continuity and discontinuity. Insofar as there is continuity, we can think by way of analogies drawn from this world. The elements of discontinuity remain inscrutable. We simply cannot grasp what goes beyond our points of reference.

Though the Bible is somewhat oblique about our future state, it is not altogether silent. We are given hints, vital clues about what the afterlife is like. There is a kind of tantalizing foretaste of future glory that is set before us, a partial unveiling that gives us a glimpse behind the dark glass. But there are a few points that are revealed to us with utmost clarity.

In this chapter, I want to examine some of the didactic assertions made about the afterlife in the Gospels and the Epistles. In the next chapter, I want us to turn our attention to the vivid images depicted in the Apocalypse of John.

THE INTERMEDIATE STATE

The Bible does not teach two states of human life, but three. There is life as we know it on earth. There is the final state of our future resurrected bodies.

And there is what happens to us between the moment of our deaths and the final resurrection. This period is known as the intermediate state.

Historically, Christian theology speaks of the intermediate state as the continued personal existence of our souls in heaven until they are reclothed with glorified bodies. In the intermediate state, we continue to exist, alive, as disembodied spirits.

The notion of soul sleep has become popular in some pockets of religion. This idea builds on the biblical use of the term *sleep* as a euphemism for death. It teaches that at death the departed souls of the saints remain in a kind of suspended animation, unconscious and unaware of the passing of time until the great resurrection. It sees an analogy between soul sleep and the sleep experiences we have in this life. When we sleep in this life, we have the sensation of the suspension of time while we are unconscious.

However, the New Testament knows nothing of soul sleep. As we have clearly seen, Paul described the intermediate state as better than this life inasmuch as we move to the immediate presence of Christ. It is difficult to imagine how that state could be better than that which we enjoy now if we remained unconscious in the presence of Christ.

Of course, there is the respite and cessation from pain and turmoil that comes from sleep, but the conscious fellowship with Christ that we presently enjoy in this life is not to be despised. There are times when we long for unconscious slumber to gain relief from the cares of this world, but the normal desire is to wake up later in order to resume conscious life. The great model of Christian bliss is not Rip Van Winkle.

The glimpses the Bible gives us of the intermediate state strongly suggest a state of alert consciousness. Though it cannot be forced too far, the parable of the rich man and Lazarus suggests a keen conscious awareness on the part of both men.

The parable involves a conversation between the rich man and Abraham. The rich man, in his torment, cried out to Abraham for mercy. Abraham replied: "Son, remember that in your lifetime you received your good things, and likewise Lazarus evil things; but now he is comforted and you are tormented. And besides all this, between us and you there is a great gulf fixed, so that those who want to pass from here to you cannot, nor can those from there pass to us" (Luke 16:25–26). Then the rich man pleaded that a message might sent to his brothers who were still alive, that they might be warned about the place of torment (vv. 27–28), but that request also was denied. In this parable, Jesus painted a picture of the "bosom of Abraham" as an intermediate place of conscious felicity and Hades as a place of conscious torment.

The vision of John recorded in the book of Revelation includes scenes of departed saints who await the final state of glory:

> When He opened the fifth seal, I saw under the altar the souls of those who had been slain for the word of God and for the testimony which they held. And they cried with a loud voice, saying, "How long, O Lord, holy and true, until You judge and avenge our blood on those who dwell on the earth?" Then a white robe was given to each of them; and it was said to them that they should rest a little while longer, until both the number of their fellow servants and their brethren, who would be killed as they were, was completed. (Rev. 6:9–11)

Here the souls of the martyrs are clearly resting in their intermediate state. But this rest is not a state of unconscious slumber. It is a conscious rest, a rest in which they are capable of conversation.

IMMEDIATELY PRESENT IN HEAVEN?

Another crucial New Testament text that bears on the issue of the intermediate state is Luke 23:43. Here Jesus spoke to the thief on the cross next to Him: "Assuredly, I say to you, today you will be with Me in Paradise."

In the original Greek text, there is no punctuation in this statement by Jesus. Specifically, no commas appear. The commas in our modern versions of the Bible are supplied by the translators. The translators of the New King James Version rendered the sense of Jesus' words in this manner—"today you shall be with Me." That is, the promise to the thief was that he would enjoy fellowship with Christ in paradise, and that fellowship would begin on that very day.

Advocates of soul sleep use a different form of punctuation. They move the comma to a different point in the sentence and render Jesus' statement in this manner: "I say to you today, you will be with Me in Paradise." In this rendition, the word *today* does not refer to the time when the thief would be with Jesus in paradise. Rather, it signifies the time when Jesus made the promise of a reunion at some point in the indefinite future.

Though this construction is grammatically possible, it is not preferred either contextually or in strict literary terms. For Jesus to take the trouble to point out what time it was when He was speaking to the thief would have been laboring the obvious. There was no point in telling the thief that "today" was the day the two men were having their conversation. If they had had a previous conversation and Jesus had said, "Someday I'm going to tell you something very important, but today is not the right time," it would have been appropriate, when the time came to reveal the important information, for Jesus to say: "All right, today is the day I'm going to tell you what I refused to reveal in the past. Today I say to you, sometime in the future you will be with me in paradise." However, there is no evidence of such a previous conversation.

This interpretation becomes all the more problematic if we consider Jesus' physical condition at the time of the utterance. He was in the midst of the agony of crucifixion, when every word He uttered required a serious effort. It seems unlikely that Jesus would have wasted His dying breath to tell the thief that He was speaking to Him "today."

The prima facie interpretation is to assume that the classical punctuation is correct. The word *today* takes on real significance if we understand Jesus to say, "I say to you, *today* you will be with Me in paradise." The words then mean, "On this very day when you are dying, on this day when you have every reason to abandon hope—on this, the last day of your earthly life—this very day will mark your entrance into a far better state than the one you are enduring at the moment. This is the day you will enter paradise."

This is the preferred rendition unless there is compelling biblical evidence

to the contrary. No such evidence exists. Indeed, that believers enter immediately into the blessed intermediate state is the consistent and harmonious
view of the rest of Scripture.

BETTER THAN LIFE ON EARTH

The New Testament leaves us with no doubt that the intermediate state is
better than life on earth. The apostle Paul declares:

> For I know that this will turn out for my deliverance through your
> prayer and the supply of the Spirit of Jesus Christ, according to my
> earnest expectation and hope that in nothing I shall be ashamed, but
> with all boldness, as always, so now also Christ will be magnified in
> my body, whether by life or by death. For to me, to live is Christ, and
> to die is gain. But if I live on in the flesh, this will mean fruit from
> my labor; yet what I shall choose I cannot tell. For I am hard pressed
> between the two, having a desire to depart and be with Christ, which is
> far better. Nevertheless to remain in the flesh is more needful for you.
> (Phil. 1:19–24)

Paul spoke of death as *gain*. We tend to think of death as *loss*. To be sure,
the death of a loved one involves a loss for those who are left behind. But for
the one who passes from this world to heaven, it is a gain.

Paul did not despise life in this world. He said that he was "hard pressed"
between the desire to remain and the desire to depart. The contrast he
pointed to between this life and heaven was not a contrast between the bad
and the good. The comparison was between the good and the better. This life
in Christ is good. Life in heaven is better. Yet Paul took it a step farther. He
declared that to depart and be with Christ is *far better* (v. 23). The transition
to heaven involves more than a slight or marginal improvement. The gain is
great. Heaven is far better than life in this world.

This echoes the comparison Paul made to the Corinthians:

For our light affliction, which is but for a moment, is working for us a far more exceeding and eternal weight of glory, while we do not look at the things which are seen, but at the things which are not seen. For the things which are seen are temporary, but the things which are not seen are eternal.

For we know that if our earthly house, this tent, is destroyed, we have a building from God, a house not made with hands, eternal in the heavens. For in this we groan, earnestly desiring to be clothed with our habitation which is from heaven, if indeed, having been clothed, we shall not be found naked. For we who are in this tent groan, being burdened, not because we want to be unclothed, but further clothed, that mortality may be swallowed up by life. Now He who has prepared us for this very thing is God, who also has given us the Spirit as a guarantee. (2 Cor. 4:17–5:5)

The contrast Paul developed here was between the temporary and the permanent, between the temporal and the eternal.

THE RESURRECTION OF THE BODY

Paul also looked to the ultimate hope of future bliss beyond the intermediate state, the third stage of human life, which includes the resurrection of our bodies. The Apostles' Creed contains the affirmation "I believe in . . . the resurrection of the body." This article of faith does not focus on the resurrection of Christ's body, but on the resurrection of our own bodies. Christ's resurrection is the precursor of our own. He is the firstfruits of all who will participate in resurrection (1 Cor. 15:20–23).

Paul elaborated the theme of our resurrected bodies in his ringing conclusion to 1 Corinthians 15: "But someone will say, 'How are the dead raised up? And with what body do they come?' Foolish one, what you sow is not made alive unless it dies. And what you sow, you do not sow that body that shall be, but mere grain—perhaps wheat or some other grain. But God gives it a body as He pleases, and to each seed its own body" (1 Cor. 15:35–38).

Paul presented an analogy drawn from agriculture. The transition we will experience between this life and the resurrection life is like that of a seed that germinates. For a seed to burst forth into life, it must first be buried. It must decay. The seed rots before the grass flowers. What emerges from the ground far exceeds in glory what was planted as a seed.

The apostle continued his analogy by referring to the wide diversity of bodies and forms by which life in this world is manifested:

All flesh is not the same flesh, but there is one kind of flesh of men, another flesh of animals, another of fish, and another of birds. There are also celestial bodies and terrestrial bodies; but the glory of the celestial is one, and the glory of the terrestrial is another. There is one glory of the sun, another glory of the moon, and another glory of the stars; for one star differs from another star in glory. (1 Cor. 15:39–41)

Paul cited a series of levels of increasing glory that are found in the created realm. He hinted of a glory that remains unseen for the present. His reasoning suggests something like this: in our limited view of the totality of reality, we glimpse but a small portion of what is actually there. We are spiritually nearsighted. It would be great arrogance to assume that life in its fullest dimension is exhausted by the scope of our limited vision. If we consider for a moment the knowledge that we have of the vast universe in which we live, we realize that the borders of our experience are infinitesimal. Our experience of the natural order is smaller than a droplet in a vast ocean. And even if we grasped the full measure of the natural order, that would not give us penetration into the supernatural realm. The lesson is this: the portion of reality we do perceive is enough to scream that there is much, much more to the diversity of life than we already experience.

Next, Paul moved to the way of contrast: "So also is the resurrection of the dead. The body is sown in corruption, it is raised in incorruption. It is sown in dishonor, it is raised in glory. It is sown in weakness, it is raised in power. It is sown a natural body, it is raised a spiritual body. There is a natural body, and there is a spiritual body" (1 Cor. 15:42–44).

The contrast between the earthly body and the resurrected body is vivid. It includes these elements:

Natural Body	Resurrected Body
Corruption	*Incorruption*
Dishonor	*Glory*
Weakness	*Power*
Natural	*Spiritual*

Corruption, dishonor, and weakness are all qualities with which we are familiar. They are a normal part of our everyday experience. They are attributes of our natural bodies. These qualities will give way in the resurrection to their antitheses. Incorruption, glory, and power are the characteristics of the spiritual body.

WHAT A SPIRITUAL BODY IS LIKE

The term *spiritual body* sounds discordant to the ear. We tend to think of spirit and body as mutually exclusive polar opposites. But Paul was not resorting to contradictions to make his point. He was referring to a spiritualized body that has been transformed from its natural limitations. It is a glorified body, a body that is raised in a new dimension.

The only real clue we have about the spiritual body is the sketchy view we have of the resurrected body of Jesus. We know that the body Jesus had after His resurrection was different than the body that was buried. His bodily resurrection manifested both continuity and discontinuity. We read of people having some difficulty recognizing Him, yet, at the same time, recognition did occur. Jesus ate breakfast with His disciples. He showed the marks of His crucifixion to Thomas. He said to him: "Reach your finger here, and look at my hands; and reach your hand here, and put it into My side. Do not be unbelieving, but believing" (John 20:27). Whether or not Thomas did as he was instructed is not recorded in the gospel, but presumably the opportunity was there for him to do it.

John also recorded a cryptic statement about Jesus that has fueled much speculation about His resurrected body: "And after eight days His disciples were again inside, and Thomas with them. Jesus came, the doors being shut, and stood in the midst, and said, 'Peace to you!'" (John 20:26).

Why did John record the phrase "the doors being shut"? Was the phrase included to tell us something about the disciples or to tell us something about the resurrected body of Jesus? On the surface, it seems like an insignificant detail. Perhaps all John had in mind was to emphasize the state of fearfulness that characterized the disciples after the crucifixion. It seems as though they spent a lot of time indoors. In verse 19 he mentioned, "When the doors were shut where the disciples were assembled, for fear of the Jews, Jesus came and stood in the midst."

We can possibly reconstruct the scene in this way: The disciples, in a state of fright, were huddled together with the doors shut. While they were preoccupied with their fear and consternation, Jesus came to their place of assembly, quietly opened the door, and came in and spoke to them. In this scenario, the reference to the shut door tells us nothing about the resurrected body of Jesus other than that it could walk around and open doors.

On the other hand, perhaps John was hinting that Jesus appeared in the middle of the room without opening the door. This would mean that His resurrected body had the capacity to move unimpeded through solid objects. The text does not explicitly say that. Such an inference is possible from the text, but it is by no means demanded from the text. It remains a matter of conjecture.

What is certain is that Paul looked to Jesus as the exemplar of what our resurrected bodies will be like:

And so it is written, "The first man Adam became a living being." The last Adam became a life-giving spirit. However, the spiritual is not first, but the natural, and afterward the spiritual. The first man was of the earth, made of dust; the second Man is the Lord from heaven. As was the man of dust, so also are those who are made of dust; and as is the heavenly Man, so also are those who are heavenly. And as we have borne the image of the man of dust, we shall also bear the image of the heavenly Man. (1 Cor. 15:45–49)

All we who are human partake of the earthly nature of Adam. We are children of the dust. Our bodies suffer from all the weaknesses and frailties that belong to the earth. Our resurrected bodies will be tabernacles made in heaven. In the heavenly body, there will be no room for cancer or heart disease. The curse of the fall will be removed. We will be clothed after the image and likeness of the new Adam, the heavenly Man. Yes, there will still be continuity. We will still be men and women. Our personal identities will remain intact. We will be recognizable as the people we were in this lifetime. But there will also be discontinuity as the shackles of the dust will be broken by the heavenly form.

CONTINUITY AND DISCONTINUITY

One vexing problem we face as we speculate about heaven is the question of recognition. We recognize people by their physical characteristics. Some of the most obvious characteristics include matters of age and weight. Will a person who dies in infancy look like a baby forever? Will the aged remain wrinkled in countenance? Will I be fat or thin, tall or short?

To ask such questions (which we can hardly resist asking) is to run head-on into the barriers of our understanding of the elements of discontinuity. I assume (and that is all it is) that somehow these questions will flee from relevance once we transcend the realm of the dust and enter into our glorified states.

Paul insisted that though we will surely maintain continuity with our present personal identities, we will nevertheless undergo transformation:

Now this I say, brethren, that flesh and blood cannot inherit the kingdom of God; nor does corruption inherit incorruption. Behold, I tell you a mystery: We shall not all sleep, but we shall all be changed—in a moment, in the twinkling of an eye, at the last trumpet. For the trumpet will sound, and the dead will be raised incorruptible, and we shall be changed. For this corruptible must put on incorruption, and this mortal must put on immortality. So when this corruptible has put on incorruption, and this mortal has put on immortality, then shall be brought to pass the saying that is written: "Death is swallowed up in victory." (1 Cor. 15:50–54)

Corruption refers to the process of death. To be corruptible in this sense does not refer to moral degeneration. It refers to physical degeneration. The process of degeneration and decay does not belong to the incorruptible. That which is free from physical corruption must escape all forms of degeneration and decay. That means that aging, wrinkles, acne, and disease have no place in that which is incorruptible. Not only death but all of death's attendants will be vanquished by the resurrection of the body.

CHAPTER TEN

A VISION OF THINGS TO COME

The most vivid and dramatic portrayal of the afterlife that we can find in Scripture is at the end of the Revelation of John. John was privileged to see, in the Spirit, a spectacular vision of the future. The culmination of John's dramatic vision is found in the unveiling of the new heaven and new earth: "Now I saw a new heaven and a new earth, for the first heaven and the first earth had passed away. Also there was no more sea" (Rev. 21:1).

Here in capsule form we see the ultimate goal of the suffering church, the culmination of God's entire plan of redemption. The future of creation is found in the manifestation of a new heaven and a new earth.

We are told that the first earth and the first heaven pass away. What does this mean? Interpreters are divided on this question. Some view the passing away of the original creation as an act of divine judgment on a fallen world. They believe the old order will be destroyed, annihilated by God's fury. Then the old will be replaced by a new act of creation. Out of nothing God will bring forth the new order.

A second view of the matter, and the one that I favor, is that the new order will involve not a new creation out of nothing but *renovation* of the old order. Its newness will be marked by God's redemption. Scripture often speaks of the entire creation awaiting the final act of redemption. To destroy something completely and to replace it with something utterly new is not an act of redemption. To redeem something is to save that which is in imminent danger of being lost. The renovation may be radical. It may involve a violent conflagration of purging, but the purifying act ultimately redeems rather than annihilates. The new heaven and the new earth will be purified. There will be no room for evil in the new order.

THE ABSENCE OF THE CHAOTIC SEA

A hint of the quality of the new heaven and new earth is found in the somewhat cryptic words, "Also there was no more sea." For people who have a love for the seashore and all that it represents in terms of beauty and recreation, it may seem strange to contemplate a new earth without any sea. But to the ancient Jew, it was a different matter. In Jewish literature, the sea was often used as a symbol for that which was ominous, sinister, and threatening. Earlier in the Revelation of John, we see the Beast emerging from the sea (Rev. 13). Likewise, in ancient Semitic mythology, there is frequent reference to the primordial sea monster that represents the shadowy chaos. The Babylonian goddess Tiamat is a case in point.

In Jewish thought, the river, the stream, or the spring functioned as the positive symbol of goodness. This was natural in a desert habitat where a stream was life itself. If we look at a relief map of Palestine, we see how crucial to the life of the land is the Jordan River. It cuts like a ribbon through the heart of an arid and parched land, connecting the Sea of Galilee in the north with the Dead Sea in the south.

The Mediterranean coast of western Palestine is marked by rocky shoals and jutting mountains. The ancient Hebrews did not develop a sea trade because the terrain was not suitable for much shipping. The sea represented trouble to them. It was from the Mediterranean that violent storms arose.

We see this contrasting imagery in Psalm 46. The psalmist writes: "God is our refuge and strength, a very present help in trouble. Therefore we will not fear, even though the earth be removed, and though the mountains be carried into the midst of the sea; though its waters roar and be troubled, though the mountains shake with its swelling" (vv. 1–3). Then he adds, "There is a river whose streams shall make glad the city of God" (v. 4).

I live in central Florida. Our area is sometimes described as "the lightning capital of America." The summer months bring severe electrical storms. My grandchildren are frequently frightened by what they call the "booming." The loud thunderclaps are not a part of what they would envision heaven to include.

But the Jews feared other problems from the sea besides turbulent storms. Their traditional archrivals, marauders who beset them countless times, were a seacoast nation. The Philistines came from the direction of the sea.

The Jew looked to a new world where all the evils symbolized by the sea would be absent. The new earth will have water. It will have a river. It will have life-giving streams. But there will be no sea there.

THE REDEEMED CITY

John continued: "Then I, John, saw the holy city, New Jerusalem, coming down out of heaven from God, prepared as a bride adorned for her husband" (Rev. 21:2). The zenith of the new order is seen in the arrival of the city of God, the redeemed Zion, the Jerusalem that descends from heaven.

The image of the city in Jewish literature is ambivalent. It oscillates between negative and positive images. On the one hand, the Jewish people were historically semi-nomadic. They moved from grazing land to grazing land. They were a people who dwelt in tents. The God of Israel was first worshiped in a tent, a tabernacle.

Yet the people longed for stability, for a sense of permanence. They rejoiced when the tabernacle gave way to a majestic temple during the reigns of David and Solomon. They were a people like the patriarch Abraham, of whom it is said: "[Abraham] dwelt in the land of promise as in a foreign country, dwelling in tents with Isaac and Jacob, the heirs with him of the same promise; *for he waited for the city which has foundations*, whose builder and maker is God" (Heb. 11:9–10, emphasis added).

Christ is celebrated in the New Testament as the great High Priest of the good things to come, "with the greater and more perfect tabernacle not made with hands, that is, not of this creation" (Heb. 9:11).

On the other hand, the image of the city in Jewish literature was negative when it represented man's arrogant attempt to create a monument to himself. It is significant that the author of Genesis mentions among the activities of the first murderer, Cain, that he built a city: "Then Cain went out from the presence of the LORD and dwelt in the land of Nod on the east of Eden. And Cain knew his wife, and she conceived and bore Enoch. And he built a city, and called the name of the city after the name of his son—Enoch" (Gen. 4:16–17). The city of Cain was unholy, just as the cities of Sodom and Gomorrah were unholy.

It was Jerusalem that became the focal point of Jewish hope. There, on Mount Zion, God promised to dwell with His people. It was there that the temple was built and to which sacred pilgrimages were made. It was up to Jerusalem that the Messiah-king had to go to die.

Israel has endured a number of holocausts, and one of the greatest took place in AD 70, when the Romans utterly destroyed the Holy City and the Jews were dispersed throughout the world. For centuries—even to this day—when the Jews celebrated the Passover, they whispered their poignant hope to one another: "Next year in Jerusalem."

Israel was the bride of Yahweh, even as the church in the New Testament is called the bride of Christ. In John's vision, the appearance of the New Jerusalem is likened to the spectacular appearance of the bride at the wedding hour. When the New Jerusalem appears, the city of man will pass away and the city of God will be ushered in.

The entrance of this city is heralded by a heavenly voice: "And I heard a loud voice from heaven saying, 'Behold the tabernacle of God is with men, and He will dwell with them, and they shall be His people. God Himself will be with them and be their God'" (Rev. 21:3).

The chief feature of the New Jerusalem will be the *immediate presence* of

God. God will be in the midst of His people. He will dwell with them. No longer will God be seen as distant, remote from everyday experience. He will pitch his tent in the midst of His people.

The closing words of Ezekiel's vision in the Old Testament capture the essence of the Holy City: "All the way around shall be eighteen thousand cubits; and the name of the city from that day shall be: THE LORD IS THERE" (Ezek. 48:35).

When John penned the prologue to his Gospel, he spoke of the Logos, the Word of God who was in the beginning with God and who was God. He wrote: "And the Word became flesh and dwelt among us, and we beheld His glory, the glory as of the only begotten of the Father, full of grace and truth" (John 1:14).

When John spoke of the incarnation, he said that the Word "dwelt" among us. The word He used literally means "pitched His tent" or "tabernacled." Jesus is called Emmanuel, meaning "God with us." The first visit of God Incarnate to Jerusalem was temporary. He came to Jerusalem and then He left Jerusalem. But He will be a permanent resident of the New Jerusalem. He will never take His leave from the Holy City. There will be no point of departure from that place.

THE END OF ALL SORROW

Continuing to describe the new heaven and earth, John wrote: "And God will wipe away every tear from their eyes; there shall be no more death, nor sorrow, nor crying. There shall be no more pain, for the former things have passed away" (Rev. 21:4).

There are few more intimate human experiences than the physical act of wiping away another person's tears. It is a tactile act of compassion. It is a piercing form of nonverbal communication. It is the touch of consolation.

When I was a child, my mother always ministered to me tenderly when I was hurt. When tears spilled out of my eyes and I sobbed with uncontrollable spasms, my mother took her handkerchief and patted the tears from my cheeks. Often she would "kiss away the tears."

My mother dried my tears more than once. Her consolation worked for the moment and my sobbing subsided. But then I would get hurt again and the tears would flow once more. Even today, many years later, my tear ducts still work. I still have the capacity to weep.

But when God will wipe away tears, it will be the end of all crying. John declared that there will be no more crying in the new earth. When God dries our eyes from all sorrowful weeping, the consolation will be permanent. There will then be no reason for mournful tears. Death will be no more. There will be no sorrow, no pain whatever. These discomforts belong to the former things that shall pass away.

The New Jerusalem will have no cemeteries. There will be no morgue, no funeral parlor, no hospital, no painkilling drugs. These are the elements that attend the travail of this world. They will all pass away.

John wrote: "Then He who sat on the throne said, 'Behold, I make all things new.' And He said to me, 'Write, for these words are true and faithful'" (Rev. 21:5).

If anything sounds too good to be true, it is the announcement of a place where pain, sorrow, tears, and death are banished. The heart almost faints at the thought of it. We are almost afraid to think of it, lest we set ourselves up for a bitter disappointment. But the commanding voice from the throne of God spoke decisively to John. "Write it down!" He ordered. "These words are true and faithful."

To call these words "true" simply means that they correspond to reality. They are not the vacuous promises of fantasy. That they are "faithful" means that they can be trusted without fear of disappointment.

John heard yet more: "And He said to me 'It is done! I am the Alpha and the Omega, the Beginning and the End. I will give of the fountain of the water of life freely to him who thirsts'" (Rev. 21:6).

The Greek alphabet begins with the letter alpha and ends with the letter omega, corresponding to our A and Z. Christ revealed Himself to John as the beginning and the end of all things. We hear the triumphant note of the victory of creation. There is no hint of an eternal cycle of meaningless repetition. There is a goal, a destiny, for all of human history. The One who creates all things brings all things to a meaningful conclusion. Vanity and futility are exiled in the light of One who is Alpha and Omega.

The One who is the Author and the Finisher of our faith promises satisfied refreshment to all who are thirsty. The powerful image of thirst appears frequently in the Scriptures. The psalmist wrote: "As the deer pants for the water brooks, so pants my soul for You, O God. My soul thirsts for God, for the living God" (Ps. 42:1–2). The human longing for God is likened to the deer whose tongue hangs out in search for water. The emotion is intense; the thirst is acute. It is to this type of person, one who has a passionate yearning for God, that Christ uttered His benediction: "Blessed are those who hunger and thirst for righteousness, for they shall be filled" (Matt. 5:6).

Jesus' words are reminiscent of His conversation with the Samaritan woman at the well: "If you knew the gift of God, and who it is who says to you, 'Give Me a drink,' you would have asked Him, and He would have given you living water. . . . Whoever drinks of the water that I shall give him will never thirst. But the water that I shall give him will become in him a fountain of water springing up into everlasting life" (John 4:10–14).

These promises reach a crescendo with the words of Jesus on the cross: "It is done!" He had accomplished His mission and the victory was assured.

John then wrote: "He who overcomes shall inherit all things, and I will be his God and he shall be My son. But the cowardly, unbelieving, abominable, murderers, sexually immoral, sorcerers, idolaters, and all liars shall have their part in the lake which burns with fire and brimstone, which is the second death" (Rev. 21:7–8).

This passage sounds an ominous note of warning. It refers to the final act of Christ's judgment. To those who are faithful comes the promise of full participation in Christ's inheritance. We are called joint heirs with Christ when we are adopted into the family of God. But those who persist in their opposition to Christ, those who ally themselves with the Antichrist, will be excluded from the felicity of heaven and consigned to the lake of fire. The catalog of sins mentioned (lying, idolatry, etc.) represents a capsule summary of the characteristics of the followers of the Antichrist who will obstinately refuse to show loyalty to Christ.

THE RADIANCE OF THE HOLY CITY

As he continued to recount his vision, John unveiled more details of the New
Jerusalem:

> Then one of the seven angels who had the seven bowls filled with the
> seven last plagues came to me and talked with me, saying, "Come, I will
> show you the bride, the Lamb's wife."
>
> And He carried me away in the Spirit to a great and high mountain,
> and showed me the great city, the holy Jerusalem, descending out of
> heaven from God, having the glory of God. Her light was like a most
> precious stone, like a jasper stone, clear as crystal. (Rev. 21:9–11)

The same angel who earlier had shown John a vision of the great harlot,
the city of Babylon (chapter 17), carried him away to see the ultimate city of
contrast. The Holy City was bathed in the refulgent glory of God. It radiated
in breathtaking brilliance. Specifically, its light was likened to a jasper stone.

Earlier in Revelation, the divine appearance on the throne was described
in these words: "And He who sat there was like a jasper and a sardius stone
in appearance" (Rev. 4:3). Jasper stones may vary in appearance from yel-
low to red to green. They may also be translucent. Sardius was red. The city
appeared to be reflecting the shekinah glory of God, transparent and fiery
red, as the light.

John continued: "Also she had a great and high wall with twelve gates,
and twelve angels at the gates, and names written on them, which are the
names of the twelve tribes of the children of Israel: three gates on the east,
three gates on the north, three gates on the south, and three gates on the
west" (Rev. 21:12–13).

In the ancient world, the strength and majesty of a city was measured by
its wall. The wall not only marked the city's boundaries, it was a vital element
of protection against enemy attack. Ancient warfare necessarily involved
the siege and the catapult in order to overcome the protection the city wall
offered. Today, visitors to the old city of Jerusalem are immediately impressed

by the wall that surrounds it. Built of great stones, the wall of Jerusalem stands seventy-five feet in height. As staggering as this sight is to the modern visitor, it is rendered even more remarkable by the fact that the erosion of time has hidden another seventy-five feet that is now underground.

However, the wall of the earthly Jerusalem will pale in comparison to that of the New Jerusalem. This wall will be great and high, indicating the total security of those who will dwell within. It will afford an impregnable barrier to any who might try to enter without the invitation of God. Yet there will be access through the twelve gates named after the twelve tribes of Israel. Salvation is of the Jews (John 4:22). The root of redemptive history is planted inside the Jewish nation. But the New Jerusalem will have gates for people from all nations to enter. Though it will honor its original nation, Israel, it will be a place where all who desire to dwell with the Lamb may enter.

Not only did John see twelve gates, he saw an equal number of foundations: "Now the wall of the city had twelve foundations, and on them were the names of the twelve apostles of the Lamb" (Rev. 21:14).

We sing of the church's one foundation being Jesus. In the New Testament imagery, however, the symbol most often used for Christ is that of the cornerstone. It is the apostles and prophets who are identified as the foundation: "Having been built on the foundation of the apostles and prophets, Jesus Christ Himself being the chief cornerstone" (Eph. 2:20).

It is significant that the wall of the New Jerusalem will rest not on one foundation but on twelve. The symmetry of twelve gates and twelve foundations symbolizing the twelve tribes of Israel and the twelve apostles shows the unity of the Old and New Testaments and the complete inclusion of all the people of God.

John's vision continued with a curious incident: "And he who talked with me had a gold reed to measure the city, its gates, and its wall. The city is laid out as a square: its length is as great as its breadth. And he measured the city with the reed: twelve thousand furlongs. Its length, breadth, and height are equal. Then he measured its wall: one hundred and forty four cubits, according to the measure of a man, that is, of an angel" (Rev. 21:15–17).

In the vision, the angel measured the Holy City with a golden instrument. The measurements revealed the perfect symmetry of the city. There were no stray lines, nothing out of balance. The city of God was perfectly plumb. We note that the city appeared to be a cube. The cube structure recalls the dimensions of the Holy of Holies in the Old Testament (see 1 Kings 6:20). Perhaps this explains a feature of the New Jerusalem that surely would have been surprising to Jews, namely that the city will have no temple in it (Rev. 21:22). The whole city will be a temple, permeated by the presence of God.

The angel found that the city measured fifteen hundred miles. The sum is symbolic. It represents the unit of the furlong multiplied by twelve. Imagine a city that extended from New York to Denver.

The measurements of the wall were also amazing. The figure of 144 cubits again represents a multiple of twelve. A cubit was originally measured as the length from a man's fingertip to his elbow. Therefore, some have estimated the wall at 216 feet.

Continuing, John noted, "The construction of its wall was of jasper; and the city was pure gold, like clear glass" (Rev 21:18).

Someone once gave me a tape that rehearsed the events that took place in the year of my birth, 1939. One of the events mentioned was the building of the Hearst mansion, which was the most elaborate and expensive private dwelling built in America up to that time. The mansion included more than a hundred rooms and cost $30 million in 1939. The gold fixtures in it were spectacular. But the Hearst mansion is a doghouse compared to the New Jerusalem.

We cannot fathom a city of pure gold that is like clear glass. We recall that Solomon's temple featured a lavish amount of gold plate. But the New Jerusalem will not be built of mere gold plate. It will feature pure gold that will radiate the beauty of God's holiness.

Returning to the city's foundations, John provided a vivid description: "The foundations of the wall of the city were adorned with all kinds of precious stones: the first foundation was jasper, the second sapphire, the third chalcedony, the fourth emerald, the fifth sardonyx, the sixth sardius, the seventh chrysolite, the eighth beryl, the ninth topaz, the tenth chrysoprase, the eleventh jacinth, and the twelfth amethyst" (Rev. 21:19–20).

The precious jewels found in the city's foundation bring to mind the jewels that adorned the breastplate of the high priest of Israel (see Ex. 28:15ff). Some have seen in them a subtle rejection of pagan religion, as John listed them in reverse order of how they function in zodiac astrology. The reality that is distorted in pagan religion is found in the city of God.

John then described the city's fabulous gates and streets: "The twelve gates were twelve pearls: each individual gate was of one pearl. And the street of the city was pure gold, like transparent glass" (Rev. 21:21).

This text is the source of the popular idea that heaven has "pearly gates" and "streets of gold." The verse recalls a prophecy found in Isaiah 54:12. The rabbis in antiquity sometimes took Isaiah's prophecy literally and looked forward to a time when Jerusalem would have pearls thirty cubits wide and twenty cubits high, with openings in them of ten by twenty cubits. (Imagine the size of the oysters that would produce such pearls.)

I was born and raised in Pittsburgh. Pittsburgh is a lovely city, far more beautiful than the popular image of a city blanketed by soot and smog from belching steel mills. The city has been on the cutting edge of urban renewal and is a model for urban renaissance. Pittsburgh's problem is not the smokestacks of the steel mills (most of which are now idle). The perennial problem that plagues the city fathers is the notorious potholes in the streets. Late winter brings a constant flux of freeze and thaw that quickly destroys the surfaces of the roads. There are legends of Volkswagens being lost forever in the cavernous chuckholes in the roads.

However, there will be no potholes in the heavenly city. There will be no road taxes necessary for constant maintenance. The streets will be paved with crystal clear gold that will never need to be resurfaced.

These graphic images are probably symbolic of the glory that will be present in heaven, though I shrink from being dogmatic about it. We ought not to put it past God to produce a city exactly as John envisioned it.

THE CITY WITHOUT A TEMPLE

As I mentioned above, there was one thing that was conspicuously absent in John's vision of the New Jerusalem. He wrote: "But I saw no temple in it, for the Lord God Almighty and the Lamb are its temple" (Rev. 21:22).

This verse would have been shocking to Jews who read it in John's time. A New Jerusalem with no temple was utterly inconceivable to them. Their future hope centered on the ultimate magnificence of the temple.

So strong was this attachment to the temple that, at His trial, Jesus' enemies twisted words He had once spoken, words that seemed to constitute a threat to the temple. A false witness said: "We heard Him say, 'I will destroy this temple made with hands, and within three days I will build another made without hands'" (Mark 14:58). Actually, Jesus had not spoken of the temple at all. When the Jews asked Him for a sign, He answered by saying:

> "Destroy this temple, and in three days I will raise it up." Then the Jews said, "It has taken forty-six years to build this temple, and will you raise it up in three days?" But He was speaking of the temple of His body. Therefore, when He had risen from the dead, His disciples remembered that He had said this to them; and they believed the Scripture and the word which Jesus had said. (John 2:19–22)

In the New Jerusalem, the temple will be replaced by the immediate presence of God the Father and the Lamb, God the Son. The risen Christ will be the "meeting place" between God and man, for He is the Mediator for His people.

Just as John saw no temple, he saw no physical source of light: "The city had no need of the sun or of the moon to shine in it, for the glory of God illuminated it. The Lamb is its light" (Rev. 21:23).

Again the words of Revelation echo the Old Testament prophecy of Isaiah: "The sun shall no longer be your light by day, nor for brightness shall the moon give light to you; but the LORD will be to you an everlasting light, and your God your glory" (Isa. 60:19).

Christ declared that He was the "light of the world" (John 8:12). In the New Jerusalem, His resurrection splendor, along with the dazzling glory of God, will dwarf the lesser luminaries of the sun and the moon.

John continued: "And the nations of those who are saved shall walk in its light, and the kings of the earth bring their glory and honor into it. Its gates shall not be shut at all by day (there shall be no night there). And they shall bring the glory and the honor of the nations into it. But there shall by no means enter it anything that defiles, or causes an abomination or a lie, but only those who are written in the Lamb's Book of Life" (Rev. 21:24–27).

The Holy City will be a place where people from all nations will flock to render tribute to the Messiah King. Earthly kings who are numbered among the redeemed will hasten to bring their own glory, riches, and honor to lay at the feet of the Lamb. The ancient magi journeyed far to offer gifts to the Christ child, but in the future there will be much more spectacular visitations of kings and princes to the throne of Christ. Then the nations will gather for worship of the King of kings. The gates will always stand open. There will be no threat of nightfall, for not a moment will pass when the splendor of the light of His presence will cease to shine.

Though the gates of the city will remain open, nothing that brings defilement will be able to pass through them. Entrance will be barred to any whose names are not written in the Lamb's Book of Life. It is the Lamb's city, so it will be open only to those who are His.

As further vistas of the city appeared in his vision, John wrote: "And he showed me a pure river of water of life, clear as crystal, proceeding from the throne of God and of the Lamb. In the middle of its street, and on either side of the river, was the tree of life, which bore twelve fruits, each tree yielding its fruit every month. The leaves of the tree were for the healing of the nations" (Rev. 22:1–2).

This scene recalls some of the elements of the Garden of Eden. We tend to think of heaven as the restoration of the Paradise that was lost in the fall. But heaven is far more than a simple restoration of the original order of things. The future paradise will far exceed the felicity that was enjoyed in the pristine Eden.

The scene also resembles the prophecy of Ezekiel:

Then he said to me: "This water flows toward the eastern region, goes down into the valley, and enters the sea. When it reaches the sea, its waters are healed. And it shall be that every living thing that moves, wherever the rivers go, will live . . . and everything will live wherever the river goes. . . . Along the bank of the river, on this side and that, will grow all kinds of trees used for food; their leaves will not wither, and their fruit will not fail. They will bear fruit every month, because their water flows from the sanctuary. Their fruit will be for food, and their leaves for medicine." (Ezek. 47:8–12)

In Ezekiel's vision, the river flows from the temple. In John's vision, it is not the temple, but Christ Himself, the Abiding Temple, who is the Source of the healing water.

In John's vision, it is difficult to determine whether he saw one tree of life with branches on both sides of the river or two separate trees of life. In either case, the tree stands for the new order of life that will be present. The annual cycle of the seasons, with birth in spring and death in winter, will be ended. The trees will bear fresh fruit every month. Their leaves will not decay and die. No more thorns or briars will be found in nature. There will be no drought to threaten the harvest.

The leaves of the trees will be therapeutic. They will contain the balm of healing for the wounds of the nations. John did not specify what maladies will be in need of healing. Perhaps he had in mind the normal pain of nature as being removed. Or he could have had in mind the healing of the wounds inflicted by the Antichrist.

THE REMOVAL OF THE CURSE

What the image of the trees only hinted at was then made explicit for John: the curse was overturned. He wrote: "And there shall be no more curse, but the throne of God and of the Lamb shall be in it, and His servants shall serve Him" (Rev. 22:3).

The idea of the curse harkens back to the fall of mankind. The curse was God's judgment on disobedience. After the fall, God cursed the Serpent who beguiled Eve. He afflicted woman with pain in childbearing and man with the added burdens of his toil. The ground was cursed with thorns (Gen. 3).

The curse motif appeared again dramatically when God made His covenant with Israel: "Behold, I set before you today a blessing and a curse: the blessing, if you obey the commandments of the LORD your God which I command you today; and the curse, if you do not obey the commandments of the LORD your God" (Deut. 11:26–28).

The curse means far more than the loss of positive blessings. Ultimately it involves being cut off from the presence of God. When Christ was crucified and "forsaken" by the Father, He was cut off from the divine presence. The lights went out, and Jesus was plunged into an abyss of darkness. The curse means that we cannot see the face of God in this world. It means that we experience a certain measure of the absence of God.

The end of the curse signals the full consummation of divine redemption. In John's vision, when the curse is removed, two things stand out immediately. The first is the clear presence of God and the Lamb. The second is the willing service rendered by His people. This stands in bold contrast to the situation that brought on the curse in the first place. The curse fell because of disobedience. When the curse is gone, there will be no more disobedience. The curse and its cause, sin, will be absent from heaven.

That, in turn, leads to the supreme hope of heaven, the vision of God. John wrote: "They shall see His face, and His name shall be on their foreheads" (Rev. 22:4).

Here is what theologians call the "beatific vision," a vision of God that provokes instant and profound joy. It is the blessedness and felicity for which everyone was created. Here the empty void that haunts the human soul will be filled at last.

There is no more difficult problem that attends the life of faith than that we are called to serve and worship a God who is utterly invisible to us. At no point is the adage "out of sight, out of mind" more keenly felt than in the object of our affections. We want to bathe our eyes in the majesty of His glory. We want Him to lift up the light of His countenance upon us. We yearn for Him to cause His face to shine upon us.

Many of the Old Testament narratives of divine appearances to human beings involve only theophanies. A theophany is a visible manifestation of the invisible God. Moses saw a bush that burned but was not consumed. The children of Israel beheld the pillar of cloud. These theophanies still maintained a veil over the face of God.

In his first epistle, the apostle John wrote: "Behold what manner of love the Father has bestowed on us, that we should be called the children of God! Therefore the world does not know us, because it did not know Him. Beloved, now we are children of God; and it has not yet been revealed what we shall be, but we know that when He is revealed, we shall be like Him, for we shall see Him as He is" (1 John 3:1–2).

John introduced this theme of the beatific vision with an expression of apostolic astonishment. He declared his profound amazement that we can be called the children of God. The bestowal of this privilege of adopted sonship reflects a "manner" or kind of love that defies all normal categories. It is a transcendent love that moves the Father to call us His children. We are categorically unworthy of such a title. The grounds for it cannot be found in any merit in us. The only possible explanation for our being called the children of God must rest in the extraordinary love that only God is capable of displaying.

John went on to confess that it has not yet been revealed what we shall be. The mirror is still dark. The future is still cloudy. But a few hints are given that are enough to set our souls on fire with delight. One thing we know for sure; one glimpse of light penetrates the darkness of the mirror—we shall be like Him.

It is ironic that we were made in God's image. The intent of God's creation of the human race was that we would mirror and reflect the very character of God. But due to our fallenness, God's image in us has been besmirched. We became lying images. There is nothing more characteristic of human beings than that we sin. In our sin, we demonstrate precisely what God is *not* like. There is no shadow of evil in the character of God.

However, when sin is altogether removed from us, then we shall be authentic images of our God. We shall be like Him.

The absolute prerequisite for beholding the face of God is purity of heart. The promise of Jesus in the Beatitudes is this: "Blessed are the pure in heart, for they shall see God" (Matt. 5:8). The reason why God is invisible to mortal men is because no mortal is pure in heart. The problem is not with our eyes; it is with our hearts.

John doesn't tell us the exact order of events. Will we first be made pure so that it will be possible to see God, or will the sight of the unveiled God instantly purify us? We know that only when we are glorified in heaven will we be qualified to see God. Therefore, I suppose that before we "see Him as He is," the residue of defilement will first be utterly cleansed from our hearts.

There is a scene in the Hollywood version of Lew Wallace's *Ben-Hur* that captures something of the poignancy of the vision of Christ. Ben-Hur is by a well, and he is filthy, stooped in the dirt, and overcome with a fierce thirst. The camera focuses on Ben-Hur's face. His countenance is twisted in misery. Then the shadow of a man crosses his visage. We do not see the man. The camera remains fixed on Ben-Hur's face. The man offers him water. As Ben-Hur lifts his wretched face to behold the merciful stranger, we see a sudden radiance transform his face. We know instantly, by the radical change of his countenance, that he is looking directly into the face of Christ.

That is the ultimate hope of the Christian. When we behold the face of God, all memories of pain and suffering will vanish. Our souls shall be totally healed.

God will put His name on our foreheads. The number of the Antichrist will not be there. We will be marked with an indelible name that will identify us forever as the sons and daughters of God.

John closed his account of his vision of the new heaven and new earth with these stirring words: "There shall be no night there: they need no lamp nor light of the sun, for the Lord God gives them light. And they shall reign forever and ever. Then he said to me, 'These words are faithful and true'" (Rev. 22:5-6a).

Once again John emphasized the banishment of all darkness. The refulgent glory of God will bathe His people in light forever. Also, those who are His will receive their full inheritance. They will hear Him say: "Come, My beloved, inherit the kingdom which has been prepared for you from the beginning of time."

It is this promise, a promise certified by the heavenly declaration, "These words are faithful and true," that removes all doubt about our present pain and suffering. It is this promise that verifies the apostolic comparison that the afflictions we endure in this life are not even worthy to be compared with the glory God has stored up for us in heaven (Rom. 8:18). It is by this promise, sealed by divine oath, that we know our suffering is never, never, never in vain.

CONCLUSION

In his letter to the Ephesians, Paul expressed the deep sentiments of his heart concerning believers:

> Therefore I also, after I heard of your faith in the Lord Jesus and your love for all the saints, do not cease to give thanks for you, making mention of you in my prayers: that the God of our Lord Jesus Christ, the Father of glory, may give to you the Spirit of wisdom and revelation in the knowledge of Him, the eyes of your understanding being enlightened; that you may know what is the hope of His calling, what are the riches of the glory of His inheritance in the saints, and what is the exceeding greatness of His power toward us who believe, according to the working of His mighty power. (Eph. 1:15–19)

In this expression of pastoral desire, Paul referred to all three of the great Christian virtues—faith, love, and hope. He exuded joy over hearing of the faith of the saints, faith that showed itself in love. But the focus of his prayer was that the Spirit of God would so illumine the minds of believers with divine wisdom that they would come to a full appreciation of the hope of His calling.

Our divine vocation is not ultimately to suffering, but to a hope that triumphs over suffering. It is the hope of our future inheritance with Christ.

This hope is no mere wish or idle longing of the soul. It is a hope that is rooted in the exceedingly great power of God. It is a hope that cannot fail. For those who embrace it, this hope will never bring shame or disappointment.

The hope of eternal joy in the presence of Christ, a hope that sustains us in the midst of temporary suffering, is the legacy of Jesus Christ. It is the promise of God to all who put their trust in Him.

QUESTIONS
AND ANSWERS

In this section, I would like to touch briefly on various other issues surrounding the problem of suffering by answering a few questions I have been asked over the years.

How would you counsel Christians who are suffering with illness or age-related infirmity and who would rather be in heaven than remain on earth?

First, I would commend such people for their preference. They are certainly in good company. Frequently this sentiment is expressed by biblical heroes and heroines. We remember the aged Simeon who, after waiting years to behold the Messiah, finally was blessed to see the Christ child in the temple. He took the baby Jesus in his arms and spoke the poem known as the *Nunc Dimittis*: "Lord, now You are letting Your servant depart in peace, according to Your word; for my eyes have seen Your salvation" (Luke 2:29–30).

Job, in the midst of his great pain, begged God for the release of death: "Oh, that I might have my request, that God would grant me the thing that

I long for! That it would please God to crush me, that He would loose His hand and cut me off!" (Job 6:8–9). Moses and Jeremiah, among others, made the same plea.

I once heard a man describing the throes of seasickness by saying, "First, I was afraid I was going to die, and then I was afraid I wouldn't." What he uttered in jest is a sober reality for many who are afflicted.

Billy Graham has been quoted publicly in recent years as saying that he was tired and longed to go home and be with Christ. Dr. Graham's remarks echoed those of the apostle Paul when he wrote: "For to me, to live is Christ, and to die is gain. But if I live on in the flesh, this will mean fruit from my labor; yet what I shall choose I cannot tell. For I am hard pressed between the two, having a desire to depart and be with Christ, which is far better. Nevertheless to remain in the flesh is more needful for you" (Phil. 1:21–24).

Paul was willing to continue his ministry on earth, but his clear preference was to die and be with Christ. Likewise, we should pray that God would give us the grace to remain fruitful in this world, even if our preference is to die and be with Christ.

There are two basic reasons why Christians at times long for death. The first is our deep longing to arrive at our spiritual destination. The pilgrimage of our souls is not finished until we enter into our rest. The second reason is the desire for relief from affliction.

As I noted earlier in this book, the time of our death is in God's hands. We must not take steps to hasten the moment of our departure. God is the author of life and is sovereign over both life and death. We may pray for death, but the request may be granted by God alone.

What about suicide? What happens to those who commit suicide?

Historically the church has taken a dim view of suicide. However, many people do, in fact, kill themselves.

I was once asked on a television talk show whether people who commit suicide could go to heaven. I answered with a simple yes. My answer caused the switchboard to light up like a Christmas tree. The host also was shocked by my response.

I explained that suicide is nowhere identified as an unforgivable sin. We do not know with any degree of certainty what is going through a person's mind at the moment of suicide. It is possible that suicide is an act of pure unbelief, a succumbing to total despair that indicates the absence of any faith in God. On the other hand, it may be the sign of temporary or prolonged mental illness. Or it may result from a sudden wave of severe depression. (Such depression can be brought on by organic causes or by the unintentional use of certain medications.)

One psychiatrist remarked that the vast majority of people who committed suicide would not have done so had they waited twenty-four hours. Such an observation is conjecture, but it is based on numerous interviews of people who made serious unsuccessful attempts at suicide and subsequently recovered from their overwhelming discouragement.

The point is that people commit suicide for a wide variety of reasons. The complexity of the thinking process of a person at the moment of suicide is known comprehensively by God alone. Therefore, God alone is able to render a fair and accurate judgment on any person. Ultimately, an individual's salvation is dependent on whether he or she has been united to Christ by faith alone. The fact remains that genuine Christians are capable of succumbing to a tidal-wave of depression.

Though we must seek to discourage people from suicide, we leave those who have done it to the mercy of God.

Can suffering in general, rather than persecution for the name of Christ, be called sharing the suffering of Christ?

I think that in some cases it can. If our suffering is done in faith, if we place our trust in God while we are suffering, then we are emulating the trust Jesus had in the Father. Certainly there is a special promise given to those who suffer unjustly. Those who are persecuted for the sake of righteousness have a host of biblical promises to comfort them.

But what if a person is suffering from an illness or some tragedy that is not a result of persecution? Here placing one's trust in God in the midst of affliction is a virtue that is not without reward. It still involves a kind of imitation of Christ. God is surely honored and pleased when His children keep the faith in the midst of suffering. In this we follow the example of Christ.

Indeed, we may also suffer as a just consequence for our sins. In this sense we are not, strictly speaking, imitating Christ, since, being perfect, He never suffered for sin. Yet even here it is possible to honor God. God was honored when the thief on the cross acknowledged that he deserved the punishment he was experiencing (Luke 23:41). He did not add blasphemy or slandering of God to the sins of which he was already guilty.

What happens to animals when they die?

This is not a frivolous question. We know that people get very attached to animals, particularly their household pets. The little girl with her kitten or the man and his dog illustrate the affection that passes between humans and animals.

Traditionally, many have been persuaded that there is no future life for animals. The Bible does not explicitly teach that animals go to heaven. One of the key arguments against the idea that animals do not survive the grave is the conviction that animals do not have souls. Many are convinced that the distinctive aspect that divides humans from animals is that humans have souls and animals do not. Some locate the image of God in man in the soul.

Likewise it is assumed that animals cannot think as we do. Their responses are explained by instinct rather than lower forms of cognition. However, the term *instinct* is a study in ambiguity. When does instinct become thought? Animals can display what we call emotion. They surely respond to external stimuli.

The Bible doesn't say that animals think. The Bible doesn't say that animals have souls. But neither does the Bible deny these things. To be sure, the Bible says the donkey knows his master's crib (Isa. 1:3). Here "knowledge" is assigned to an animal. However, the passage could be interpreted metaphorically or poetically, so we remain uncertain.

One thing we are sure of: biblically, redemption is spelled out in cosmic terms. Just as the whole creation was plunged into ruin by the fall of man, so the whole creation groans together, awaiting redemption: "For the earnest expectation of the creation eagerly waits for the revealing of the sons of God. For the creation was subjected to futility, not willingly, but because of Him who subjected it in hope; because the creation itself also will be delivered from the bondage of corruption into the glorious liberty of the children of God" (Rom. 8:19–21).

Images of heaven and future redemption include animals. The lamb, the lion, and the wolf are all mentioned. Again, these images may be only metaphorically illustrative. But coupled with the promise of cosmic redemption, they lend some real hope to the future redemption of man's animal companions.

Is it wrong to try to avoid suffering?

There have been times in church history when suffering was looked on as such a virtue that people went out of their way to experience it. The ancient heresy of Manichaeism, which focused on releasing the soul from the evil flesh, had a powerful and lasting influence on the church. Rigorous acts of asceticism, including bizarre forms of self-flagellation, have been seen as ways of accruing merit in the sight of God.

However, suffering merely for the sake of suffering has no particular virtue. The quest for suffering may indicate a psychological disorder, such as masochism. It also may point to an attempt at self-justification whereby a person, out of pride, wants to atone for his sins rather than to receive the grace of forgiveness.

There is no reason to seek suffering. Neither is there anything wrong in trying to avoid it unless avoiding it purposely involves a betrayal of Christ. The early martyrs could have avoided the lions if they had repudiated Christ, but such an avoidance of suffering would have been sin. Such examples are not limited to the early church. In many situations in the contemporary world, notably in totalitarian countries, Christians choose—and in some cases do not choose—to suffer for Christ.

We seek to avoid suffering when we buy food to eat and use medicine to heal our diseases. This is not sin but prudence. God calls us to take care of ourselves in the stewardship of both body and soul.

So the avoidance of suffering may be virtue or sin, depending on the circumstances involved.

When a baby dies or is aborted, where does its soul go?

The way this question is worded indicates a certain ambiguity about the relationship between abortion and death. If life begins at conception, then abortion is a type of death. If life does not begin until birth, then obviously abortion does not involve death. The classical view is that life begins at conception. If that is so, the question of infant death and prenatal death involve the same answer.

Any time a human being dies before reaching the age of accountability (which varies according to mental capacity), we must look to special provisions of God's mercy. Most churches believe that there is such a special provision in the mercy of God. This view does not involve the assumption that infants are innocent. David declared that he was both born in sin and conceived in sin (Ps. 51:5). By this he was obviously referring to the biblical notion of original sin. Original sin does not refer to the first sin of Adam and Eve, but to the result of that initial transgression. Original sin refers to the condition of our fallenness, and it affects all human beings. We are not sinners because we sin; rather, we sin because we are sinners. That is, we sin because we are born with sinful natures.

Though infants are not guilty of actual sin, they are tainted with original sin. That is why we insist that the salvation of infants depends not on their presumed innocence but on God's grace.

My particular church believes that the children of believers who die in infancy go to heaven by the special grace of God. What happens to the children of unbelievers is left to the realm of mystery. There may be a special provision of God's grace for them as well. We can certainly hope for that.

Even though we hope for such grace, there is little specific biblical teaching on the matter. Jesus' words, "Let the little children come to Me; for of such is the kingdom of heaven" (Matt. 19:14), give us some consolation but do not offer a categorical promise of infant salvation.

When the son of David and Bathsheba was taken by God, David lamented, "While the child was alive, I fasted and wept; for I said, 'Who can tell whether the LORD will be gracious to me, that the child may live?' But now he is dead; why should I fast? Can I bring him back again? *I shall go to him*, but he shall not return to me" (2 Sam. 12:22–23, emphasis added).

Here David declared his confidence that "I shall go to him." Though this could have referred merely to David's eventual death, it is more likely a thinly veiled reference to his hope of future reunion with his son. This hope of a future reunion is a glorious hope, one that is buttressed by the New Testament teaching on the resurrection.

Does free will play a role in suffering? For example, if a man smokes and then dies from cancer, is his suffering a call from God as a vocation? Is it a divine judgment? Or is it a result of the man taking his chances?

This question lists three possible explanations for the suffering described. We can eliminate one of them altogether. If God is sovereign, then nothing happens purely by chance. A chance event would be totally outside of the sovereign will of God. If any events were outside the sovereign will of God, it would be a contradiction in terms to call God sovereign. As I've written elsewhere, if there is one maverick molecule in the universe running around free of God's sovereignty, then there is no guarantee that any promise God has ever made will come to pass. That one molecule might be the very thing that disrupts God's eternal plan. Not just the best-laid plans of mice and men, but those of the Creator himself, might go astray.

If God is not sovereign, then God is not God. A non-sovereign God is no God at all. A non-sovereign God would be like a titular king who reigns but doesn't rule. To be sure, men have free will, but our free will is limited. It is always limited by God's free will. God's free will is a sovereign free will. Our free will is a subordinate free will.

When I speak of suffering being a vocation, I have in mind that God is sovereign over everything that happens to us. That does not cancel out our free will and responsibility.

The question remains, is the suffering mentioned the result of God's vocation or God's judgment? Here we face a false dilemma. This need not be an either/or situation. God's call to suffer may at the same time be an act of judgment.

We remember the nocturnal call that came to Samuel when he served under Eli. God revealed to Samuel that He was going to bring His holy judgment on the house of Eli. Eli then begged Samuel to tell him what God had revealed: "'What is the word that the LORD spoke to you? Please do not hide it from me. God do so to you, and more also, if you hide anything from me of all the things that He said to you.' Then Samuel told him everything, and hid nothing from him. And he said, 'It is the LORD. Let Him do what seems good to Him'" (1 Sam. 3:17–18).

Eli recognized the judgment of God. He recognized the justice of it. He submitted himself to it. Here he accepted a vocation, a call to bear a chastisement involving suffering.

Likewise, when Nathan told David that David had sinned, David repented. David's life was spared, but his son's was not: "So David said to Nathan, 'I have sinned against the LORD.' And Nathan said to David, 'The LORD also has put away your sin; you shall not die. However, because by this deed you have given great occasion to the enemies of the LORD to blaspheme, the child also who is born to you shall surely die'" (2 Sam. 12:13–14).

The biblical record informs us that David then pleaded with God for the child. He fasted and prayed. But God said no. On the seventh day, the child died. What was David's response? "So David arose from the ground, washed and anointed himself, and changed his clothes; and he went into the house of the LORD and worshiped" (2 Sam. 12:20).

David worshiped God in the midst of his suffering. Indeed, he knew he was suffering under the corrective judgment of God. David answered the call of God righteously.

David's response echoes that of Job when Job declared: "Naked I came from my mother's womb, and naked shall I return there. The LORD gave, and the LORD has taken away; blessed be the name of the LORD" (Job 1:21).

How do you explain the out-of-body, "tunnel-like" experiences that many people have reported after being revived from death?

I can't offer a full explanation for this phenomenon. There has been a significant amount of research on this, but the results are, at best, speculative. I've heard reports claiming that as many as 50 percent of those who have suffered clinical death and have been resuscitated through CPR or other means report some strange experience. Some report the sensation of looking down from the ceiling and seeing their own body lying in the bed while doctors or nurses were making ministrations. Some have reported moving through a vast tunnel bathed in a brilliant light.

Most of these reports have been of a positive nature. Others, however, have reported frightening and ominous experiences that gave them pause about what might be awaiting them beyond the veil.

Religious interpretations of these experiences are complicated by the fact that the same positive experiences have been reported by believers and unbelievers alike.

Various explanations for these phenomena have been offered. One involves a type of hallucination potential brought on by medication or short circuits in the brain similar to the explanation often given for *déjà vu* experiences. Another explanation is based on the biblical affirmation of life after death. As Christians, we believe that the soul survives death. There is a continuity of personal existence after the cessation of physical life. Whether we're good or bad, redeemed or unredeemed, the life of the soul continues.

I'm fascinated by these reports and look forward to future scientific analysis of them. I keep before me, however, the parable of the rich man and Lazarus, in which the warning is uttered, "If they do not hear Moses and the prophets, neither will they be persuaded though one rise from the dead" (Luke 16:31).

Why do people attempt to contact the dead through mediums? Do such attempts actually work?

We long for concrete, tangible proof that life continues after death. We want the assurance that someone has gone beyond and has come back, or at least has given us a message from the other side. But attempts to reach such assurance through illegitimate means are fraught with perils.

The practice of necromancy, commonly called "spiritualism," demonstrates mankind's profound desire to gain firsthand information from the other side. The séances of the spiritualist promise such information via the trappings of medium communication, table rappings, and the appearance of ghostly shapes of ectoplasm.

The Old Testament calls such activity an abomination to God. It was a capital crime in the nation of Israel. The New Testament is as opposed to sorcery and magic as the Old Testament, as we see from the apostolic confrontation of such practices in the book of Acts.

It is interesting that the Bible records a story in which the spirit of the prophet Samuel supposedly was summoned by the witch of Endor at the behest of King Saul (1 Sam. 28). The narrative certainly sounds like it was a genuine contact with someone who was dead. But was it?

I see three possible ways to understand this narrative. First, it may be a record of a satanic miracle. In other words, the witch may have summoned Samuel by the power of Satan. The Bible attributes to Satan the power of performing "signs, and lying wonders" (2 Thess. 2:9). However, the accent here is not on the word *wonders* but on the qualifying adjective *lying*. Satan does not perform real miracles but fraudulent ones. In any case, God holds the keys of death, not Satan. Even if Satan had the ability to perform real miracles, he could not exercise that power where God does not permit him to do so.

Second, the narrative may simply be a faithful record of the event as it appeared. The Bible frequently uses what we call "phenomenological" language, language that describes events *as they appear to the naked eye*. Under this scenario, the apparent summoning of Samuel may simply have been a cleverly devised trick that Saul saw as real.

Third, the narrative here may be presenting a description of a real medium-conjured summoning of a spirit. The Bible does not absolutely affirm that Samuel was really called up from death, but it does not deny it either. However, even if the witch actually did summon Samuel, her success does not endorse the practice of spiritualism. The witch of Endor was guilty of practicing something that, fraudulent or real, was a capital offense in Israel.

It is my belief that the summoning of Samuel did not really happen but that it was a clever trick. I believe the witch of Endor was a fraud, and I think the same is true of all such mediums. It is beyond dispute that many spiritualists have been exposed as frauds, but none have been authenticated.

If we desire confirmation for life after death, there is a better place to look for it than in the realm of magic or the occult. We can go beyond the speculation of philosophers, the mumbo-jumbo of the occultists, and the legerdemain of the illusionists. We can go to the New Testament, to the words and work of Jesus. His words transcend the fraudulent and bring us into the realm of sober, historical truth, and His works (His miracles) authenticate His words.

INDEX
OF SCRIPTURE

INDEX OF SUBJECTS
AND NAMES

ABOUT THE AUTHOR

Dr. R.C. Sproul was founder of Ligonier Ministries, founding pastor of Saint Andrew's Chapel in Sanford, Fla., first president of Reformation Bible College, and executive editor of *Tabletalk* magazine. His radio program, *Renewing Your Mind*, is still broadcast daily on hundreds of radio stations around the world and can also be heard online.

He was author of more than one hundred books, including *The Holiness of God*, *Chosen by God*, and *Everyone's a Theologian*. He was recognized throughout the world for his articulate defense of the inerrancy of Scripture and the need for God's people to stand with conviction upon His Word.